Gems of Guidance

D1596053

Gems of Guidance

*Selections from the Scriptures
of the World*

compiled and introduced

by

David Jurney

GEORGE RONALD
OXFORD

GEORGE RONALD, Publisher
46 High Street, Kidlington, Oxford OX5 2DN

This compilation © David Jurney 1992
All Rights Reserved

A CIP record for this book is available
from the British Library.

ISBN 0–85398–348–8
ISBN 0-85398–349–6 Pbk

Printed and bound
in Great Britain

Contents

Dedicated to my beloved wife Vedad and our dear sons Nabil and Riaz, and to all the people in the world who are making an effort to work for world peace

Acknowledgements

I would like to thank all those people who have assisted me in compiling and writing this book. My wife, Vedad, has been especially helpful and encouraging during the time it has taken to put *Gems of Guidance* into its present form. I would like to express my appreciation to Dr Jean Scales and Mr Larry Miller for offering helpful suggestions, and to Mrs Pam Altman for her skilful word processor production of the manuscript.

An Ancient Love Story

You are invited to learn about a unique love story, the oldest love story in the world. It is the story of God's love for humankind. Just as loving, caring parents do everything they can to guide and assist their children, God provides guidance and assistance for humanity. Thousands of years ago God made a covenant with Abraham that He would never leave the world without guidance. Since the time of that covenant history has recorded great advances of civilization.

If the people who lived in the time of Abraham could see today's world, they would probably consider the new inventions and scientific discoveries as miraculous; but after closer observation they would agree that the greatest miracle witnessed by humankind during this long period of history has been the fulfilment of God's promise to provide guidance for humanity. One source of this guidance is the sacred writings of the major religions of the world. These writings are like paintings of unexcelled beauty. An attempt has been made in this book to choose from the vast number of these master-pieces a select few and to arrange them so that you will enjoy their inspiring verses. Some of the writings quoted are very ancient, and others are as recent as the twentieth century.

The sacred writings of these religions provide inspira-tion and guidance while addressing thousands of subjects related to our lives. God in His wisdom knows our strengths and our weaknesses, our hopes and our fears. The chapters on creation, prayer, meditation, faith, unity and love are subjects familiar to millions of people of different religious beliefs throughout the world.

You may not understand all the concepts in these sacred writings without further study, but there are many things which are easily comprehended. Look for the beauty and inspiration in these scriptures and do not burden yourself by looking up the definition of every unknown word. If a selection is confusing to you, turn to one that you can understand, or first read selections from the scriptures of your own religion and then compare them with the selections from the other religions on the same subject.

The main theme of this book is the guidance which the sacred writings of six major religions of the world provide for people like you and me. Recent surveys have shown that a large percentage of people in the United States believe they receive guidance and assistance from God. People from many parts of the world with different religious and cultural backgrounds share this belief in guidance. The sacred writings of the religions tell us to knock, to search and to seek guidance and assistance from God. The creation of God is so beautiful, and the universe functions so magnificently with the planets, moons and stars spinning through space in exact orbits. The pattern of God's creation, which causes mighty oaks to grow from tiny acorns and birds to migrate thousands of miles each year to raise their young, is a wonder to behold. The same God who created the universe with the flowers, tropical birds and butterflies also provides the religions with their prophet-founders and sacred writings. These writings show another part of the beauty of God's creation.

Guidance and assistance from God are subjects of interest to many people. As we read what the sacred writings of the different religions have to say about specific subjects, we become aware of the close kinship of all the major religions. By learning more about the religions, we gain a better understanding of people throughout the world. A peaceful world is a goal that most people cherish in their hearts. As we acquire more knowledge of the religions and the people of the world, we move one step closer to world peace.

Gems of Guidance

The following chapters contain excerpts from the sacred writings and teachings of the Hindu, Buddhist, Jewish, Christian, Islamic and Bahá'í religions. The sacred writings and teachings quoted here represent only a small part of the ocean of knowledge provided for our guidance. The Prophets of God and the religions they establish are a part of the pattern of creation. We have the opportunity to seek out the guidance provided in the sacred writings of these religions for our own development and for the advancement of civilization. History records our progress on this planet as we respond to an innate need to strive to higher and higher degrees of perfection. As we move forward, each generation has a larger knowledge base to build upon and the potential to develop deeper levels of consciousness and understanding. God has created humanity to move forward, and the sacred writings and teachings of the religions provide guidance and inspiration to help make this progress possible.

Creation

The sacred writings of the religions tell us that God created the universe and the spiritual worlds beyond. We become aware of the perfect order of the universe when we study the planetary systems. The stars, planets and moons move through space in predetermined orbits. Our planet earth, a very small segment of the universe, is part of the Creator's complex and perfect design. Geologists tell us that the age of the earth is between five hundred million and two billion years old. The earth went through a long period of cooling and development during which an atmosphere was gradually formed. This was followed by simple forms of plants and animals which have evolved into the complex and diverse forms that we witness on the earth today. Humankind is like a beautiful butterfly emerging from a cocoon – after millions of years of development humanity has attained its present stage of perfection. As we study, we discover that humankind has continued to advance from prehistoric times through the long period of recorded history until the present. During the past six thousand years man has made tremendous progress. The ancient Hebrews thought they were at the centre of the universe and that the sun, moon and stars revolved around them. Today we have extensive knowledge of our own galaxy and astronomers speak of one hundred million other galaxies.

How can we not be overwhelmed by contemplating the perfect creation of God?

When we study the history of humanity we see the human race moving towards higher and higher forms of social unity. From the family, people came together and formed tribes. As humanity progressed, cities and later city-states were organized. In the seventh century history records the beginning of nationhood. Today humankind moves forward towards a higher form of unity: global unity and world peace. God did not create the universe to stand still. He created a system which incorporates movement, development and progress. Each generation of humanity witnesses this forward movement. The progress varies in different cultures and in different parts of the world, but the overall picture records progress during every period of history. If some segments of humanity seem at a standstill or seem to be regressing, many other segments of humanity are moving forward. The process of development and movement applies to the whole universe, but we are more clearly aware of the progress we see on this planet.

We become impatient sometimes because we are in the primary school stage of the development of humankind when we would like to be in the high school or college stage of the process. We long for the age of maturity when all people can live together on this planet in peace and harmony. The religions and their prophet-founders have had, and are having, a great influence on the people of the world.

God created the universe and all things therein. He created the physical and spiritual elements. As we

search and study we become more aware of the infinite
magnitude and the perfect order of God's creation.

Gems
from the
Hindu Teachings

By Me, Unmanifest in form,
This whole universe was spun:
In Me subsist all beings,
I do not subsist in them.

And (yet) contingent beings do not subsist in Me –
Behold my sovereign power (yoga)!
My Self sustains (all) beings, it does not subsist in
    them;
It causes them to be.

As in (wide) space subsists the mighty wind,
Blowing (at will) ever and everywhere,
So too do all contingent beings
Subsist in Me: so must thou understand.

All contingent beings pass
Into material Nature which is Mine
When an aeon comes to an end; and then again
When another aeon starts, I emanate them forth.

Firm-fixed in my material Nature
Ever again I emanate

This whole mighty host of beings,
Powerless themselves – from Nature comes the
  power.

These works of mine
Bind Me not nor limit Me:
As one indifferent I sit
Among these works, detached.

(A world of) moving and unmoving things
Material Nature brings to birth, while I look on and
  supervise:
This is the cause and this the means
By which the world revolves.

For that a human form I have assumed
Fools scorn Me,
Knowing nothing of my higher nature (bhāva) –
Great Lord of (all) contingent beings.[1]

Bhagavad-Gita

Gems
from the
Buddhist Teachings

And as all things originate from one Essence, so they
are developing according to one law, and they are
destined to one aim, which is Nirvana . . .[2]

Dhammapada

And the Buddha said, 'The Tathagata sees the universe face to face and understands its nature. He proclaims the truth both in its letter and in its spirit, and his doctrine is glorious in its origin, glorious in its progress, glorious in its consummation.'[3]

Tevijja Sutta

Gems
from the
Jewish Teachings

In the beginning God created the heaven and the earth.[4]

Genesis

When I behold Thy heavens, the work of Thy fingers, The moon and the stars, which Thou has established; What is man, that Thou are mindful of him? And the son of man, that Thou thinkest of him? Yet Thou hast made him but little lower than the angels, And hast crowned him with glory and honour. Thou hast made him to have dominion over the works of Thy hands; Thou hast put all things under His feet: Sheep and oxen, all of them, Yea, and the beasts of the field; The fowl of the air, and the fish of the sea; Whatsoever passeth through the paths of the seas. O Lord, our Lord, How glorious is Thy name in all the earth.[5]

Psalms

Gems
from the
Christian Teachings

I am Alpha and Omega, the beginning and the ending, saith the Lord, which is, and which was, and which is to come, the Almighty.[6]

Revelation

In the beginning was the Word, and the Word was with God, and the Word was God. The same was in the beginning with God. All things were made by him; and without him was not any thing made that was made. In him was life; and the life was the light of men.[7]

St John

Gems
from the
Islamic Teachings

Of God it is to point out 'the Way'. Some turn aside from it: but had He pleased, He had guided you all aright. It is He who sendeth down rain out of Heaven: from it is your drink; and from it are the plants by which ye pasture. By it He causeth the corn, and the olives, and the palmtrees, and the grapes to spring forth for you, and all kinds of fruits: verily, in this are signs for those who ponder. And He hath subjected to you the night and the day; the sun and the moon and the stars too are subjected to you by his behest; verily, in this are signs for those who understand: And all varied hues that He hath created for you over the earth: verily, in this are signs for those who remember. And He it is who hath subjected the sea to you, that ye may eat of its fresh fish, and take forth from it ornaments to wear – thou seest the ships ploughing its billows – and that ye may go in quest of His bounties, and that ye might give thanks. And He hath thrown firm mountains on the earth, lest it move with you; and rivers and paths for your guidance, and way marks. By the stars too are men guided. Shall He then who hath created be as he who hath not created? Will ye not consider? And if ye would reckon up the favours of God, ye could not count them. Aye! God is right Gracious, Merciful! And God knoweth what ye conceal, and what ye bring to light . . .[8]

Qur'án

Of what ask they of one another?
Of the great news.
The theme of their disputes.
Nay! they shall certainly know its truth!
Again. Nay! they shall certainly know it.
Have we not made the Earth a couch?
And the mountains its tent-stakes?
We have created you of two sexes,
And ordained your sleep for rest,
And ordained the night as a mantle,
And ordained the day for gaining livelihood,

And built above you seven solid heavens,
And placed therein a burning lamp;
And we send down water in abundance from the
   rain-clouds,
That we may bring forth by it corn and herbs,
And gardens thick with trees.[9]

Qur'án

It is God who hath given you the earth as a sure
foundation, and over it built up the Heaven, and formed
you, and made your forms beautiful, and feedeth you
with good things. This is God your Lord. Blessed then
be God the Lord of the Worlds!

   He is the Living One. No God is there but He. Call
then upon Him and offer Him a pure worship. Praise be
to God the Lord of the Worlds![10]

Qur'án

No defect canst thou see in the creation of the God of
Mercy: Repeat the gaze: seest thou a single flaw?[11]

Qur'án

Gems
from the
Bahá'í Teachings

The one true God hath everlastingly existed, and will
everlastingly continue to exist. His creation, likewise,

hath had no beginning, and will have no end. All that is
created, however, is preceded by a cause. This fact, in
itself, establisheth, beyond the shadow of a doubt, the
unity of the Creator.

Thou hast, moreover, asked Me concerning the
nature of the celestial spheres. To comprehend their
natures it would be necessary to inquire into the
meaning of the allusions that have been made in the
Books of old to the celestial spheres and the heavens,
and to discover the character of their relationship to
this physical world, and the influence which they exert
upon it. Every heart is filled with wonder at so be-
wildering a theme, and every mind is perplexed by its
mystery. God, alone, can fathom its import. The
learned men, that have fixed at several thousand years
the life of this earth, have failed, throughout the long
period of their observation, to consider either the
number or the age of the other planets. Consider,
moreover, the manifold divergencies that have resulted
from the theories propounded by these men. Know
thou that every fixed star hath its own planets, and
every planet its own creatures, whose number no man
can compute.[12]

Bahá'u'lláh

All-praise to the unity of God, and all-honour to Him,
the sovereign Lord, the incomparable and all-glorious
Ruler of the universe, Who, out of utter nothingness,
hath created the reality of all things, Who, from
naught, hath brought into being the most refined and
subtle elements of His creation, and Who, rescuing His
creatures from the abasement of remoteness and the

perils of ultimate extinction, hath received them into
His kingdom of incorruptible glory. Nothing short of
His all-encompassing grace, His all-pervading mercy,
could have possibly achieved it. How could it, other-
wise, have been possible for sheer nothingness to have
acquired by itself the worthiness and capacity to
emerge from its state of non-existence into the realm of
being?

Having created the world and all that liveth and
moveth therein, He, through the direct operation of
His unconstrained and sovereign Will, chose to confer
upon man the unique distinction and capacity to know
Him and to love Him – a capacity that must needs be
regarded as the generating impulse and the primary
purpose underlying the whole of creation . . . Upon the
inmost reality of each and every created thing He hath
shed the light of one of His names, and made it a
recipient of the glory of one of His attributes. Upon the
reality of man, however, He hath focused the radiance
of all of His names and attributes, and made it a mirror
of His own Self. Alone of all created things man
hath been singled out for so great a favour, so enduring
a bounty.[13]

Bahá'u'lláh

Prayer

Prayer is an important part of the teachings of all religions. The sacred writings of these religions tell us that prayer is communion with God. Prayer can become a spiritual force to help bring assistance or greater awareness. How many times have we heard the expression 'prayer changes things'? The revealed prayers and inspirational writings from the sacred texts of the religions reflect beauty comparable to the writings of the world's greatest poets, and they are endowed with spiritual qualities transcending all other forms of literature. Prayers are revealed in these writings for assistance, unity, families, healing, and for acquiring spiritual qualities. We are encouraged to pray for our own development, for our families and for all humankind. When we pray sincerely, new levels of consciousness are attained. As we read and memorize the verses of these sacred writings we become aware of the special 'power of the Word' which they contain. This is one of the reasons that the sacred writings of the religions are protected and preserved for thousands of years. We become aware of the influence they can have on our lives and on the progress of civilization.

Prayer is the key for opening doors to deeper levels of consciousness. It assists the individual to become aware of his or her proper relationship to God. We are told to seek, to knock, and to ask for assistance. Those who believe in the power of prayer are well aware how

many of their prayers have been answered. All the
Prophets of God have devoted a portion of their time to
prayer and meditation. We have the recorded words of
these Prophets which have been preserved for our use.
There is no need to ask whether or not these Prophets
believed in the power of prayer. Their example teaches
us how we can establish our own relationship to God as
we pray.

In this chapter selections have been made from the
sacred writings which tell of the importance of prayer
and the wisdom of praying. These selections are
followed by prayers and inspirational verses from these
sacred writings.

Gems
from the
Hindu Teachings

O Father of the Earth, by fixed laws ruling,
O Father of the Heavens, pray protect us,
O Father of the great and shining Waters!
What God shall we adore with our oblation?

O Lord of creatures, Father of all beings,
You alone pervade all that has come to birth.
Grant us our heart's desire for which we pray.
May we become the lords of many treasures![1]

Rig-Veda

Draw near in friendship.
Save us and help us.
Show yourself gracious, O Lord!

Be present, O Lord,
Wonderful, adorned.
Shower on us treasure most precious!

Hear now our cry.
Lend us your ear.
Shield us from sin's contagion!

To you, radiant God,
We bring this prayer.
Shine on our friends in blessing![2]

Rig-Veda

Breathe on us fearlessness, Heaven and Earth!
By the Strength of God,
by the Light of God,
may we be free from fear!
May the boundless atmosphere set us in fearlessness!
May the offering of the seven Seers set us in
    fearlessness!

From the North and the South, the East and the
    West,
let the Light of God
direct on this village

sustenance, welfare, and ease.
May the Power of God grant us freedom from foes,
removing all fear, deflecting all wrath.

Below and above,
behind and before,
grant us freedom from enemies, O Power of God.[3]

Atharva-Veda

Gems
from the
Buddhist Teachings

And now, Ananda, stand up, facing westward, and
having taken a handful of flowers, fall down. This is the
quarter where that Bhagovat Amitabha, the Tathagata,
holy and fully enlightened, dwells, remains, supports
himself and teaches the Law, whose spotless and pure
name, famed in every quarter of the whole world with
its ten quarters, the blessed Buddhas, equal to the sand
of the river Ganga, speaking and answering again and
again without stopping, extol, praise and eulogize.[4]

Sukhavati-Vyuha

Calm is the mind, calm is the speech, and action and
right knowledge of him who is wholly freed, perfectly
peaceful, and who is such a stable one.[5]

Dhammapada

Gems
from the
Jewish Teachings

O give thanks unto the Lord, call upon His name;
Make known His doings among the peoples. Sing unto
Him, sing praises unto Him; Speak ye of all His
marvellous works. Glory ye in His holy name; Let the
heart of them rejoice that seek the Lord. Seek ye the
Lord and His strength; Seek His face continually.[6]

Psalms

God be gracious unto us, and bless us; May He cause
His face to shine toward us; Selah. That Thy way may
be known upon earth, Thy salvation among all nations.
Let the peoples give thanks unto Thee, O God; Let the
peoples give thanks unto Thee, all of them. O let the
nations be glad and sing for joy; For Thou wilt judge
the peoples with equity, And lead the nations upon
earth. Selah. Let the peoples give thanks unto Thee, O
God; Let the peoples give thanks unto Thee, all of
them. The earth hath yielded her increase; May God,
our own God, bless us. May God bless us; And let all
the ends of the earth fear Him.[7]

Psalms

Create in me a clean heart, O God; And renew a
steadfast spirit within me. Cast me not away from Thy
presence; And take not Thy holy spirit from me.

Restore unto me the joy of Thy salvation; And let a willing spirit uphold me.[8]

Psalms

The Lord bless thee, and keep thee; The Lord make His face to shine upon thee, and be gracious unto thee; The Lord lift up His countenance upon thee, and give thee peace.[9]

Numbers

Unto Thee, O Lord, do I lift up my soul. O my God, in Thee have I trusted, let me not be ashamed; Let not mine enemies triumph over me. Yea, none that wait for Thee shall be ashamed; They shall be ashamed that deal treacherously without cause. Show me Thy ways, O Lord; Teach me Thy paths. Guide me in Thy truth, and teach me; For Thou art the God of my salvation; For Thee do I wait all the day. Remember, O Lord, Thy compassions and Thy mercies; For they have been from of old.[10]

Psalms

Gems
from the
Christian Teachings

. . . Ask, and it shall be given you; seek, and ye shall find; knock, and it shall be opened unto you. For every one that asketh receiveth; and he that seeketh findeth;

and to him that knocketh it shall be opened.[11]

St Luke

Our Father which art in heaven, Hallowed be thy name.
Thy kingdom come. Thy will be done in earth, as it is in
heaven. Give us this day our daily bread. And forgive us
our debts, as we forgive our debtors. And lead us not into
temptation, but deliver us from evil: For thine is the kingdom, and the power, and the glory, for ever. Amen.[12]

St Matthew

Blessed are the poor in spirit: for theirs is the kingdom
of heaven. Blessed are they that mourn: for they shall
be comforted. Blessed are the meek: for they shall
inherit the earth. Blessed are they which do hunger and
thirst after righteousness: for they shall be filled. Blessed
are the merciful: for they shall obtain mercy. Blessed are
the pure in heart: for they shall see God. Blessed are the
peacemakers: for they shall be called the children of
God . . . Let your light so shine before men, that they
may see your good works, and glorify your Father
which is in heaven.[13]

St Matthew

Gems
from the
Islamic Teachings

Enjoin prayer on thy family, and persevere therein. We
ask not of thee to find thine own provision – we will

provide for thee, and a happy issue shall there be to
piety.[14]

Qur'án

Therefore remember me: I will remember you; and
give me thanks and be not ungrateful.

O ye who believe! seek help with patience and with
prayer, for God is with the patient.[15]

Qur'án

O my son! verily God will bring everything to light,
though it were but the weight of a grain of mustard-
seed, and hidden in a rock or in the heavens or in the
earth; for, God is subtle, informed of all.

O my son! observe prayer, and enjoin the right and
forbid the wrong, and be patient under whatever shall
betide thee: for this is a bounden duty.[16]

Qur'án

Praise be to God, Lord of the worlds!
The compassionate, the merciful!
King on the day of reckoning!
Thee only do we worship, and to Thee do we cry for
    help.
Guide Thou us on the straight path,
The path of those to whom Thou hast been gracious –
with whom thou art not angry, and who go not astray.[17]

Qur'án

SAY: God sufficeth me: in Him let the trusting trust.[18]

Qur'án

Gems
from the
Bahá'í Teachings

Intone, O My servant, the verses of God that have been received by thee, as intoned by them who have drawn nigh unto Him, that the sweetness of thy melody may kindle thine own soul, and attract the hearts of all men. Whoso reciteth, in the privacy of his chamber, the verses revealed by God, the scattering angels of the Almighty shall scatter abroad the fragrance of the words uttered by his mouth, and shall cause the heart of every righteous man to throb. Though he may, at first, remain unaware of its effect, yet the virtue of the grace vouchsafed unto him must needs sooner or later exercise its influence upon his soul. Thus have the mysteries of the Revelation of God been decreed by virtue of the Will of Him Who is the Source of power and wisdom.[19]

Bahá'u'lláh

The wisdom of prayer is this: That it causeth a connection between the servant and the True One, because in that state man with all heart and soul turneth his face towards His Highness the Almighty, seeking His association and desiring His love and compassion. The greatest happiness for a lover is to converse with his beloved, and the greatest gift for a seeker is to become familiar with the object of his longing; that is why with every soul who is attracted to the Kingdom of God, his greatest hope is to find an opportunity to entreat and supplicate before his Beloved, appeal for His mercy and grace and be immersed in the ocean of His utterance, goodness and generosity.[20]

'Abdu'l-Bahá

We should speak in the language of heaven – in the language of the spirit – for there is a language of the spirit and heart. It is as different from our language as our own language is different from that of the animals, who express themselves only by cries and sounds.

It is the language of the spirit which speaks to God. When, in prayer, we are freed from all outward things and turn to God, then it is as if in our hearts we hear the voice of God. Without words we speak, we communicate, we converse with God and hear the answer . . . All of us, when we attain to a truly spiritual condition, can hear the Voice of God.[21]

'Abdu'l-Bahá

Know thou of a certainty that every house wherein the anthem of praise is raised to the Realm of Glory in celebration of the Name of God is indeed a heavenly home, and one of the gardens of delight in the Paradise of God.[22]

'Abdu'l-Bahá

The traditions established the fact that in all Dispensations the law of prayer hath constituted a fundamental element of the Revelation of all the Prophets of God

– a law the form and the manner of which hath been adapted to the varying requirements of every age.[23]

Bahá'u'lláh

O my God! O my God! Unite the hearts of Thy servants, and reveal to them Thy great purpose. May they follow Thy commandments and abide in Thy law. Help them, O God, in their endeavour, and grant them strength to serve Thee. O God! Leave them not to themselves, but guide their steps by the light of Thy knowledge, and cheer their hearts by Thy love. Verily, Thou art their Helper and their Lord.[24]

Bahá'u'lláh

From the sweet-scented streams of Thine eternity give me to drink, O my God, and of the fruits of the tree of Thy being enable me to taste, O my Hope! From the crystal springs of Thy love suffer me to quaff, O my Glory, and beneath the shadow of Thine everlasting providence let me abide, O my Light! Within the meadows of Thy nearness, before Thy presence, make me able to roam, O my Beloved, and at the right hand of the throne of Thy mercy, seat me, O my Desire! From the fragrant breezes of Thy joy let a breath pass over me, O my Goal, and into the heights of the paradise of Thy reality let me gain admission, O my Adored One! To the melodies of the dove of Thy oneness suffer me to hearken, O Resplendent One, and through the spirit of Thy power and Thy might quicken me, O my Provider! In the spirit of Thy love keep me steadfast, O my Succorer, and in the path of Thy good

pleasure set firm my steps, O my Maker! Within the
garden of Thine immortality, before Thy countenance,
let me abide for ever, O Thou Who art merciful unto
me, and upon the seat of Thy glory stablish me, O Thou
Who art my Possessor! To the heaven of Thy loving-
kindness lift me up, O my Quickener, and unto the
Daystar of Thy guidance lead me, O Thou my Attrac-
tor! Before the revelations of Thine invisible spirit
summon me to be present, O Thou Who art my Origin
and my Highest Wish, and unto the essence of the
fragrance of Thy beauty, which Thou wilt manifest,
cause me to return, O Thou Who art my God!

  Potent art Thou to do what pleaseth Thee. Thou art,
verily, the Most Exalted, the All-Glorious, the All-
Highest.[25]

Bahá'u'lláh

Is there any Remover of difficulties save God? Say:
Praised be God! He is God! All are His servants, and
all abide by His bidding![26]

The Báb

Blessed is the spot, and the house, and the place, and
the city, and the heart, and the mountain, and the
refuge, and the cave, and the valley, and the land, and
the sea, and the island, and the meadow where mention
of God hath been made, and His praise glorified.[27]

Bahá'u'lláh

Meditation

In the sacred writings of the religions we discover the words prayer and meditation frequently used together. The two activities are often closely associated with each other. In prayer we make statements, supplicate, or ask for assistance. In meditation we ponder, reflect, contemplate, or listen in silence for inspiration. Many books have been written on the subject of meditation. The Prophets of God have revealed verses and encouraged us to read and ponder on the deeper meaning of these verses. When we read about the lives of the Prophets we see how they practised meditation and spiritual attunement. Some of the Prophets withdrew to the mountains or the wilderness for periods of prayer and reflection.

Meditation may be silent contemplation of a prayer or other inspirational verse. At times we might use this form of meditation to solve a problem or for inspiration in perfecting a work of art. Another form of meditation is to empty the mind during a period of silence. This allows the deeper levels of the mind to assist us. This same type of assistance or deeper understanding may come to us in our dreams: we let the mind relax and, during sleep, perhaps the answer we have been seeking will come in a dream which we recall upon awakening.

'Meditate', 'ponder', 'contemplate' and 'reflect' are words we often encounter as we read the sacred

writings of the religions. We are encouraged to use
meditation in our daily lives. Through meditation we
can discover bounties and deeper understandings which
we may not be able to receive in any other way. As we
begin to devote some time each day to meditation, we
realize why it should be an important part of our plan
for making spiritual progress.

In this chapter selections have been made from the
sacred writings of the different religions which describe
the importance of meditation. These are followed by
verses from the sacred writings which may be used as
inspiration for meditation. Included are only a few
priceless pearls out of a vast ocean which is filled with
bounties awaiting our discovery.

Gems
from the
Hindu Teachings

Meditation (dhyāna) is greater than thought. The earth
seems to meditate; atmosphere and sky seem to meditate; the waters and the mountains seem to meditate, as
do gods and men. That is why whenever men achieve
greatness on earth, they may be said to have received
their (due) portion of the fruits of meditation. So, while
small men are quarrelsome, slanderous gossips, the
great may be said to have received their (due) portion of
the fruits of meditation. Revere meditation.[1]

Chandogya Upanishad

Let a man's thoughts be integrated with the discipline
   (yoga)
Of constant striving: let them not stray to anything
   else (at all);
So by meditating on the divine All-Highest Person,
(That man to that All-Highest) goes.

For (He it is who is called) the Ancient Seer,
Governor (of all things, yet) smaller than the small,
Ordainer of all, in form unthinkable,
Sun-coloured beyond the darkness. Let a man
   meditate on Him (as such).[2]

Bhagavad-Gita

Who sends the mind to wander afar? Who first drives
life to start on its journey? Who impels us to utter these
words? Who is the Spirit behind the eye and the ear?

It is the ear of the ear, the eye of the eye, and the
Word of words, the mind of mind, and the life of life.
Those who follow wisdom pass beyond and, on leaving
this world, become immortal.

There the eye goes not, nor words, nor mind. We
know not, we cannot understand, how he can be
explained: He is above the known and he is above the
unknown. Thus have we heard from the ancient sages
who explained this truth to us.

What cannot be spoken with words, but that whereby
words are spoken: Know that alone to be Brahman, the
Spirit; and not what people here adore.

What cannot be thought with the mind, but that
whereby the mind can think: Know that alone to be
Brahman, the Spirit; and not what people here adore.

What cannot be seen with the eye, but that whereby
the eye can see: Know that alone to be Brahman, the
Spirit; and not what people here adore.

What cannot be heard with the ear, but that whereby
the ear can hear: Know that alone to be Brahman, the
Spirit; and not what people here adore.

What cannot be indrawn with breath, but that whereby breath is indrawn: Know that alone to be Brahman,
the Spirit; and not what people here adore.[3]

Kena Upanishad

Gems
from the
Buddhist Teachings

Wake up! It is time to wake up!
You are young, strong – why do you waver,
why are you lazy and irresolute?
This is not the way to wisdom.

Be strict with speech, control your mind,
let not the body do evil.
This is the way to wisdom,
these the three roads leading to it.

Meditation brings wisdom,
lack of meditation is folly.
These are the two roads,
one leading forward, one backwards.

Choose the right one,
the one that leads to wisdom.

Not one tree – cut down the whole forest!
There is danger in the forest.
Cut down the forest of desires, O bhikkus,
and discover the road to liberation.[4]

Dhammapada

Forbearing patience is the highest devotion . . .[5]

Dhammapada

Though one should live a hundred years, without
wisdom and control, yet better, indeed, is the single
day's life of one who is moral and meditative.[6]

Dhammapada

Clear thinking leads to Nirvana
A confused mind is a place of death.
Clear thinkers do not die,
the confused ones have never lived.

The wise man appreciates clear thinking,
delights in its purity, and
selects it as the means to Nirvana.

He meditates, he perseveres,
he works hard for the incomparable freedom and
    bliss of Nirvana.

He steps forward:
this clear thinker and pure worker,
this dignified and disciplined disciple of Dhamma.

Clear thinking, right action, discipline and restraint
make an island for the wise man,
an island safe from floods.

Sloth is loved by the ignorant and foolish;
the wise man's treasure is his clear thinking.

'Never sloth, never lust, never the senses' –
This is clear thinking, which brings great joy.

Suppressing sloth steadily, slowly,
a man climbs the tower of serene wisdom.
Sees, below, the suffering multitudes,
as one from a high hill sees the level plain.

While others sleep he is awake,
they sleep, he works.
He is the wise man,
the race horse swiftly advancing.

Clear thinking made Indra chief god.
Let us praise clear thinking, confusion canceller.

For it moves like a flame, burning
all bondage, big and small.
A bhikku with clear thinking sees confusion clearly,
and is not afraid.

A bhikku with clear thinking is close to Nirvana.
He sees confusion clearly, and is not afraid.[7]

Dhammapada

Who runs after pleasure and shuns meditation,
losing himself in the delights of the world,
envies the man who prefers meditation.

Give up both pleasant and unpleasant!
Missing the pleasant is pain, and
finding the unpleasant is also pain.

To lose what one loves is pain.
For which reason, control the senses.
Only he is free who neither likes nor dislikes.

Liking brings grief,
Liking brings fear.
The man who curbs liking is free from grief
and free from fear.

Affection brings grief,
affection brings fear.
The man who curbs affection is free from grief
and free from fear.

Desire brings grief,
desire brings fear.
The man who curbs desire is free from grief
and free from fear.

Craving brings grief,
craving brings fear.
The man who curbs craving is free from grief
and free from fear.

Dear to the world is the man
who is truthful, virtuous, and discriminating,
who pursues his own business, which is devotion to
    Dhamma.

Only he crosses the stream of life
who wishes to know what is known as Unknowable,
who is lord of his senses and filled with dedication.

When, after a long journey a man returns home,
safely – kinsmen, friends, and well-wishers rejoice.

So, when a man travels from this birth to the next,
his good deeds rejoice, waiting like kinsmen to
    receive a friend.[8]

Dhammapada

One should learn virtue which is of extensive goal,
And (which hath) the faculty of Happiness;
And one should devote oneself to Charity,
To tranquil behaviour (samacariya) and to thoughts
    of Friendship.

Having devoted himself to these three virtues,
Which provide reason for happiness,

A wise man gaineth the world of happiness –
A world free from distress.[9]

Buddha

Gems
from the
Jewish Teachings

This book of the law shall not depart out of thy mouth, but thou shalt meditate therein day and night, that thou mayest observe to do according to all that is written therein; for then thou shalt make thy ways prosperous, and then thou shalt have good success. Have not I commanded thee? Be strong and of good courage; be not affrighted, neither be thou dismayed: for the Lord thy God is with thee whithersoever thou goest.[10]

Joshua

Let the words of my mouth and the meditation of my heart be acceptable before Thee, O Lord, my Rock, and my Redeemer.[11]

Psalms

Happy is the man that hath not walked in the counsel of the wicked, Nor stood in the way of sinners, Nor sat in the seat of the scornful. But his delight is in the law of the Lord; And in His Law doth he meditate day and night. And he shall be like a tree planted by streams of water, That bringeth forth its fruit in its season, And whose leaf doth not wither; And in whatsoever he doeth he shall prosper.[12]

Psalms

The Lord is my shepherd; I shall not want. He maketh me to lie down in green pastures; He leadeth me beside the still waters. He restoreth my soul; He guideth me in straight paths for His name's sake. Yea, though I walk through the valley of the shadow of death, I will fear no evil, For Thou art with me; Thy rod and Thy staff, they comfort me. Thou preparest a table before me in the presence of mine enemies; Thou hast anointed my head with oil; my cup runneth over. Surely goodness and mercy shall follow me all the days of my life; And I shall dwell in the house of the Lord for ever.[13]

Psalms

Shout unto the Lord, all the earth. Serve the Lord with gladness; Come before His presence with singing. Know ye that the Lord He is God; It is He that hath made us, and we are His, His people, and the flock of His pasture. Enter into His gates with thanksgiving, And into His courts with praise; Give thanks unto Him, and bless His name. For the Lord is good; His mercy endureth for ever; And His faithfulness unto all generations.[14]

Psalms

I will lift up mine eyes unto the mountains: From whence shall my help come? My help cometh from the

Lord, Who made heaven and earth. He will not suffer
thy foot to be moved; He that keepeth thee will not
slumber. Behold, He that keepeth Israel doth neither
slumber nor sleep. The Lord is thy keeper; The Lord is
thy shade upon thy right hand. The sun shall not smite
thee by day, Nor the moon by night. The Lord shall
keep thee from all evil; He shall keep thy soul. The
Lord shall guard thy going out and thy coming in. From
this time forth and for ever.[15]

Psalms

Gems
from the
Christian Teachings

Finally, brethren, whatsoever things are true, whatsoever things are honest, whatsoever things are just,
whatsoever things are pure, whatsoever things are
lovely, whatsoever things are of good report; if there be
any virtue, and if there be any praise, think on these
things.[16]

Philippians

If any of you lack wisdom, let him ask of God, that
giveth to all men liberally, and upbraideth not; and it
shall be given him. But let him ask in faith, nothing
wavering. For he that wavereth is like a wave of the sea
driven with the wind and tossed. For let not that man

think that he shall receive any thing of the Lord. A double minded man is unstable in all his ways.[17]

St James

And as ye would that men should do to you, do ye also to them likewise.[18]

St Luke

But the fruit of the Spirit is love, joy, peace, longsuffering, gentleness, goodness, faith, meekness, temperance: against such there is no law.[19]

Galatians

Ye have heard that it hath been said, Thou shalt love thy neighbour, and hate thine enemy. But I say unto you, Love your enemies, bless them that curse you, do good to them that hate you, and pray for them which despitefully use you, and persecute you; that ye may be the children of your Father which is in heaven: for he maketh his sun to rise on the evil and on the good, and sendeth rain on the just and on the unjust. For if ye love them which love you, what reward have ye? do not even the publicans the same? And if ye salute your brethren only, what do ye more than others? do not even the publicans so? Be ye therefore perfect, even as your Father which is in heaven is perfect.[20]

St Matthew

And he said, Whereunto shall we liken the kingdom of God? or with what comparison shall we compare it? It

is like a grain of mustard seed, which, when it is sown in
the earth, is less than all the seeds that be in the earth:
But when it is sown, it groweth up, and becometh
greater than all herbs, and shooteth out great branches;
so that the fowls of the air may lodge under the shadow
of it.[21]

St Mark

Gems
from the
Islamic Teachings

A blessed Book have we sent down to thee, that men
may meditate its verses, and that those endued with
understanding may bear it in mind.[22]

Qur'án

Each hath a succession of Angels before him and behind
him, who watch over him by God's behest. Verily, God
will not change his gifts to men, till they change what is in
themselves . . .[23]

Qur'án

He is God beside whom there is no god: He is the King,
the Holy, the Peaceful, the Faithful, the Guardian, the
Mighty, the Strong, the Most High! Far be the Glory of
God from that which they unite with Him!

He is God, the Producer, the Maker, the Fashioner! To Him are ascribed excellent titles. Whatever is in the Heavens and in the Earth praiseth Him. He is the Mighty, the Wise![24]

Qur'án

And they who believe on God and his Apostles, and make no difference between them – these! we will bestow on them their reward at last. God is Gracious, Merciful![25]

Qur'án

We created man: and we know what his soul whispereth to him, and we are closer to him than his neck-vein.

When the two angels charged with taking account shall take it, one sitting on the right hand, the other on the left:

Not a word doth he utter, but there is a watcher with him ready to note it down . . .[26]

Qur'án

Gems
from the
Bahá'í Teachings

Meditate profoundly, that the secret of things unseen may be revealed unto you, that you may inhale the sweetness of a spiritual and imperishable fragrance, and that you may acknowledge the truth that from time immemorial even unto eternity the Almighty hath tried, and will continue to try, His servants, so that light may be distinguished from darkness, truth from falsehood, right from wrong, guidance from error, happiness from misery, and roses from thorns.[27]

Bahá'u'lláh

Bahá'u'lláh says there is a sign (from God) in every phenomenon: the sign of the intellect is contemplation and the sign of contemplation is silence, because it is impossible for a man to do two things at one time – he cannot both speak and meditate.

It is an axiomatic fact that while you meditate you are speaking with your own spirit. In that state of mind you put certain questions to your spirit and the spirit answers: the light breaks forth and the reality is revealed.

You cannot apply the name 'man' to any being void of this faculty of meditation; without it he would be a mere animal, lower than the beasts.

Through the faculty of meditation man attains to eternal life; through it he receives the breath of the Holy Spirit – the bestowal of the Spirit is given in reflection and meditation.

The spirit of man is itself informed and strengthened during meditation; through it affairs of which man knew nothing are unfolded before his view. Through it he receives Divine inspiration, through it he receives heavenly food.

Meditation is the key for opening the doors of mysteries. In that state man abstracts himself: in that state man withdraws himself from all outside objects; in that subjective mood he is immersed in the ocean of spiritual life and can unfold the secrets of things-in-themselves. To illustrate this, think of man as endowed with two kinds of sight; when the power of insight is being used the outward power of vision does not see.

This faculty of meditation frees man from the animal nature, discerns the reality of things, puts man in touch with God.

This faculty brings forth from the invisible plane the sciences and arts. Through the meditative faculty inventions are made possible, colossal undertakings are carried out; through it governments can run smoothly. Through this faculty man enters into the very Kingdom of God.

Nevertheless some thoughts are useless to man; they are like waves moving in the sea without result. But if the faculty of meditation is bathed in the inner light and characterized with divine attributes, the results will be confirmed.

The meditative faculty is akin to the mirror; if you put it before earthly objects it will reflect them. Therefore if the spirit of man is contemplating earthly subjects he will be informed of these.

But if you turn the mirror of your spirits heavenwards, the heavenly constellations and the rays of the Sun of Reality will be reflected in your hearts, and the virtues of the Kingdom will be obtained.

Therefore let us keep this faculty rightly directed – turning it to the heavenly Sun and not to earthly objects – so that we may discover the secrets of the Kingdom, and comprehend the allegories of the Bible and the mysteries of the spirit.

May we indeed become mirrors reflecting the heavenly realities, and may we become so pure as to reflect the stars of heaven.[28]

'Abdu'l-Bahá

God has sent forth the Prophets for the purpose of quickening the soul of man into higher and divine recognitions. He has revealed the heavenly Books for this great purpose. For this the breaths of the Holy Spirit have been wafted through the gardens of human hearts, the doors of the divine Kingdom opened to mankind and the invisible inspirations sent forth from on high. This divine and ideal power has been bestowed upon man in order that he may purify himself from the imperfections of nature and uplift his soul to the realm of might and power. God has purposed that the darkness of the world of nature shall be dispelled and the imperfect attributes of the natal self be effaced in the effulgent reflection of the Sun of Truth. The mission of the Prophets of God has been to train the souls of humanity and free them from the thralldom of natural instincts and physical tendencies. They are like unto Gardeners, and the world of humanity is the field of Their cultivation, the wilderness and untrained jungle growth wherein They proceed to labour.[29]

'Abdu'l-Bahá

O my brother! A divine Mine only can yield the gems of divine knowledge, and the fragrance of the mystic

Flower can be inhaled only in the ideal Garden, and the lilies of ancient wisdom can blossom nowhere except in the city of a stainless heart.[30]

Bahá'u'lláh

Heed not your weaknesses and frailty; fix your gaze upon the invincible power of the Lord, your God, the Almighty. Has He not, in past days, caused Abraham, in spite of His seeming helplessness, to triumph over the forces of Nimrod? Has He not enabled Moses, whose staff was His only companion, to vanquish Pharaoh and his hosts? Has He not established the ascendancy of Jesus, poor and lowly as He was in the eyes of men, over the combined forces of the Jewish people? Has He not subjected the barbarous and militant tribes of Arabia to the holy and transforming discipline of Muḥammad, His Prophet? Arise in His name, put your trust wholly in Him, and be assured of ultimate victory.[31]

The Báb

Faith

Faith means unquestioning belief and complete trust or confidence. The sacred writings of the religions encourage us to have faith in God. An unquestioning belief in God may be obtained through a personal spiritual experience. Others achieve this faith by studying the sacred writings of the religions and others through prayer and meditation. The study of the perfect order of the universe and the planet we live on has convinced many people that the creation must have a creator. If we have attained faith in God we will need to continue acquiring knowledge throughout our lives to maintain and strengthen our faith.

The Prophets of God are inspired to reveal teachings to assist us in building our faith. The sacred writings of these religions repeatedly remind us of God's presence, of His assistance, and His concern for humanity and for each of us. We are told that if we have as much faith as a tiny mustard seed then we will be assisted by God. Faith must be built on conscious knowledge. We might wish to pray for the sun to rise an hour earlier tomorrow morning, but if we are aware of the physical laws of the universe and the solar system we will not expect this prayer to be answered. We need to become aware of the physical and spiritual laws which are functioning in our daily lives. As we learn more about these laws our faith in God can be built on knowledge.

In these sacred writings we are told that science and

religion must agree. Truth is one and cannot be
divided. As we advance we continue to discover new
physical and spiritual laws. We find ourselves in a
process of learning more about the earth we live on,
our solar system and our galaxy. Our thinking must
continually readjust to the knowledge we acquire; new
discoveries, inventions and ideas have to be assimi-
lated. As our knowledge base grows larger, our faith in
God must continue to expand, incorporating newly-
acquired information and life experience. The sacred
writings of the religions can strengthen our faith in God
as we become more aware of the gifts and bounties
which His creation has provided for us.

Gems
from the
Hindu Teachings

Whoso shall practise constantly
This my doctrine, firm in faith,
Not envying (not cavilling),
He too shall find release from (the bondage that is)
   work.

But whoso refuses to perform my doctrine,
Envious (yet, and cavilling),
Of every (form of) wisdom fooled,
Is lost, the witless (dunce)! Be sure of that.

As is a man's own nature,
So must he act, however wise he be.

All beings follow Nature:
What can repression do?

In all the senses passion and hate
Are seated, (turned) to their proper objects:
Let none fall victim to their power,
For these are brigands on his road.[1]

Bhagavad-Gita

By Faith is Fire kindled.
By Faith is offered Sacrifice.
Sing we now Faith, the pinnacle of joy.

Bless Faith, the one who gives.
Bless him who wills, but has not.
Bless him who gives his worship unstinting.
Bless this song I sing.

As the Gods evoked Faith
from the mighty Asuras,
so may my prayer for the generous worshipper be
   accepted!

The Gods, led by the Spirit,
honour Faith in their worship.
Faith is composed of the heart's intention.
Light comes through Faith.

Through Faith men come to prayer,
Faith in the morning.
Faith at noon and at the setting of the Sun.
O Faith, give us Faith![2]

Rig-Veda

A man of faith, intent on wisdom,
His senses (all) restrained, will wisdom win;
And, wisdom won, he'll come right soon
To perfect peace.

The man, unwise, devoid of faith,
Doubting at heart (atman), must perish:
No part in this world has the man of doubt,
Nor in the next, nor yet in happiness.

Let a man in spiritual exercise (yoga) all works
    renounce,
Let him by wisdom his doubts dispel,
Let him be himself (ātmavat) and then
(Whatever) his works (may be), they will never bind
    him (more).

And so, (take up) the sword of wisdom, cut
This doubt of thine, unwisdom's child,
Still lurking in thy heart:
Prepare for action (now), stand up![3]

Bhagavad-Gita

Gems
from the
Buddhist Teachings

The man of faith is revered wherever he goes:
he has virtue and fame, he prospers.

Good men shine, even from a distance,
like the Himalaya mountains,
but the wicked, like arrows shot in the night, fade
  away.

Sit alone, sleep alone, be active alone,
in loneliness continue the conquest of the self,
even in a forest continue the quest.[4]

Dhammapada

Let us live happily,
hating none though others hate.
Let us live without hate among those who hate.

Let us live happily,
free from disease, among the diseased.
Let us live diseaseless among the diseased.

Let us live happily,
ungrieving among others who grieve.
Let us live without grief among those who grieve.

Let us live happily, without possessions.
Let us feed on happiness like the shining gods.

Victory breeds hate; the defeated will grieve.
Who goes beyond victory and defeat is happy.

No fire like passion,
no sickness like hate,
no grief like the ego's
and no joy like peace.

No disease like greed,
no sorrow like desire.

He who knows this
is fit for Nirvana.

No gift like health,
no wealth like calm of mind,
no faith like trust,
no peace like Nirvana.[5]

Dhammapada

Gems
from the
Jewish Teachings

In Thee, O Lord, have I taken refuge; let me never be
ashamed; Deliver me in Thy righteousness. Incline
Thine ear unto me, deliver me speedily; Be Thou to me
a rock of refuge, even a fortress of defence, to save me.
For Thou art my rock and my fortress; Therefore for
Thy name's sake lead me and guide me. Bring me forth
out of the net that they have hidden for me; For Thou
art my stronghold. Into Thy hand I commit my spirit;
Thou hast redeemed me, O Lord, Thou God of truth.[6]

Psalms

. . . And He will teach us of His ways, And we will
walk in His paths; For out of Zion shall go forth the
law, and the word of the Lord from Jerusalem. And He
shall judge between many peoples, And shall decide
concerning mighty nations afar off; And they shall beat

their swords into plowshares, And their spears into pruning hooks; Nation shall not lift up sword against nation, Neither shall they learn war any more. But they shall sit every man under his vine and under his fig tree; And none shall make them afraid; For the mouth of the Lord of hosts hath spoken. For let all the peoples walk each one in the name of its god, But we will walk in the name of the Lord our God for ever and ever.[7]

Micah

Gems
from the
Christian Teachings

. . . for verily I say unto you, If ye have faith as a grain of mustard seed, ye shall say unto this mountain, Remove hence to yonder place; and it shall remove; and nothing shall be impossible unto you.[8]

St Matthew

Consider the lilies how they grow: they toil not, they spin not; and yet I say unto you, that Solomon in all his glory was not arrayed like one of these. If then God so clothe the grass, which is to day in the field, and to morrow is cast into the oven; how much more will he clothe you, O ye of little faith? And seek not ye what ye shall eat, or what ye shall drink, neither be ye of doubtful mind. For all these things do the nations of the world seek after: and your Father knoweth that ye have need of these things. But rather seek ye the kingdom of God; and all these things shall be added unto you.[9]

St Luke

Jesus said unto him, If thou canst believe, all things are possible to him that believeth.[10]

St Mark

And be not conformed to this world: but be ye transformed by the renewing of your mind, that ye may prove what is that good, and acceptable, and perfect, will of God. For I say, through the grace given unto me, to every man that is among you, not to think of himself more highly than he ought to think; but to think soberly, according as God hath dealt to every man the measure of faith.[11]

Romans

Now faith is the substance of things hoped for, the evidence of things not seen.[12]

Hebrews

Gems
from the
Islamic Teachings

How can ye withhold faith from God? Ye were dead and He gave you life; next He will cause you to die;

next He will restore you to life: next shall ye return to Him!

He it is who created for you all that is on Earth, then proceeded to the Heaven, and into seven Heavens did He fashion it: and He knoweth all things.[13]

Qur'án

It is God who hath reared the Heavens without pillars thou canst behold; then mounted his throne, and imposed laws on the sun and moon: each travelleth to its appointed goal. He ordereth all things. He maketh his signs clear, that ye may have firm faith in a meeting with your Lord.[14]

Qur'án

Gems
from the
Bahá'í Teachings

Oh, trust in God! for His Bounty is everlasting, and in His Blessings, for they are superb. Oh! put your faith in the Almighty, for He faileth not and His goodness endureth for ever! His Sun giveth Light continually, and the Clouds of His Mercy are full of the Waters of Compassion with which He waters the hearts of all who trust in Him. His refreshing Breeze ever carries healing in its wings to the parched souls of men![15]

'Abdu'l-Bahá

Moreover, a soul of excellent deeds and good manners will undoubtedly advance from whatever horizon he beholdeth the lights radiating. Herein lies the difference: By faith is meant, first, conscious knowledge, and second, the practice of good deeds.[16]

'Abdu'l-Bahá

Unity

Unity means being joined together in harmony and love. This concept can refer to an individual who is unified within himself or herself, or to a unified world. The history of the world shows that people have become united in larger and larger groups. Pre-historic man lived in caves and hunted for meat, wild fruit and berries to feed his family. At a later time groups of people united to form tribes. This tribal concept continued for thousands of years into the period of recorded history. Following the development of agriculture, villages and later towns were built. As towns became larger they became cities. Later, cities grouped together into city-states. The next step in uniting large numbers of people under one government took place when nation-states were established, and in recent history nations in various parts of the world have formed alliances based on common goals.

In the twentieth century we are fortunate to live at a time when world unity is a possibility. The means for travel to all parts of the world in a short period of time are now available. The development of the telegraph, telephone, radio, television and communication satellites has created a world communication system, which provides one of the necessary steps for bringing about world peace.

The sacred writings of the religions have furnished guidelines for moral and legal standards for thousands of years. As we read the verses of these sacred writings we discover some of the things we can do as individuals to help bring about world peace. We are encouraged to love all humanity and to overcome all forms of religious, racial, class, national and cultural prejudices. We are told to overcome religious fanaticism and indifference toward the less fortunate people of the world. We are asked to found strong, peaceful, united families which can form the basis of strong, peaceful, united communities. Education for all the people in the world will play an important role in bringing about a just and lasting world peace. As humankind develops spiritually and intellectually, we move closer to achieving the universal peace and unity about which the Prophets of God have written.

Gems
from the
Hindu Teachings

For seeing Him the same, the Lord,
Established everywhere,
He cannot of himself to (him)self do hurt;
Hence he treads on the highest Way.

Nature it is which in every way
Does works (and acts);
No agent is the self: who sees it thus,
He sees indeed.

When once a man can see that (all) the diversity
Of contingent beings abides in One (alone),
And from That alone they radiate,
Then to Brahman he attains.

Because this All-Highest Self knows no beginning,
No quality, it passes not away;
Though abiding in (many a) body,
He does not act nor is He defiled.

Just as the ether, roving everywhere,
Knows no defilement, so subtle (is its essence),
So does this Self, though everywhere abiding
And embodied, know no defilement.

As the one sun lights up
This whole universe,
So does the 'Knower of the field'
Illumine (this) whole 'field'.

Whoso with wisdom's eye discerns the difference
Between 'field' and 'Knower of the field',
And knows deliverance from beings in their material
    (prakrti) form,
Treads on the highest Way.[1]

Bhagavad-Gita

The integrated man, renouncing the fruit of works,
Gains an abiding peace:
The man not integrated, whose works are prompted
    by desire,
Holds fast to fruits and thus remains enslaved.

(And so,) all works renouncing with his mind,
Quietly he sits in full control
Within (this) body, city of nine gates:
He neither works nor makes another work.

Nor agency nor worldly works
Does (the body's) lord engender,
Nor yet the bond that work to fruit conjoins;
It is Nature (svabhāva) that initiates the action.[2]

Bhagavad-Gita

Of one heart and one mind I make you,
devoid of hate.
Love one another, as a cow
loves the calf she has borne.

Let the son be courteous to his father,
of one mind with his mother.
Let the wife speak words that are gentle
and sweet to her husband.

Never may brother hate brother
or sister hurt sister.
United in heart and in purpose,
commune sweetly together.

I will utter a prayer for such concord
among family members
as binds together the Gods,
among whom is no hatred.

Be courteous, planning and working
in harness together.
Approach, conversing pleasantly
like-minded, united.

Have your eating and drinking in common.
I bind you together.
Assemble for worship of the Lord,
like spokes around a hub.[3]

Atharva-Veda

Gems
from the
Buddhist Teachings

All beings tremble before danger, all fear death.
  When a man considers this, he does not kill or
  cause to kill.

All beings fear before danger, life is dear to all.
  When a man considers this, he does not kill or
  cause to kill.

He who for the sake of happiness hurts others who
  also want happiness, shall not hereafter find
  happiness.

He who for the sake of happiness does not hurt
  others who also want happiness, shall hereafter
  find happiness.

Never speak harsh words, for once spoken they may
  return to you. Angry words are painful and there
  may be blows for blows.

If you can be in silent quietness like a broken gong
  that is silent, you have reached the peace of
  Nirvana and your anger is peace.[4]

Dhammapada

Regard thy people as men do an only son. Do not
oppress them, do not destroy them; keep in due check
every member of thy body, forsake unrighteous doctrine and walk in the straight path. Exalt not thyself by
trampling down others, but comfort and befriend the
suffering.[5]

Buddhacarita

Walk, monks, on tour for the blessing of the many, for
the happiness of the many, out of compassion for the
world, for the welfare, the blessing, the happiness of
devas (gods) and men.[6]

Vinaya-pitaka

Just as with her own life a mother shields from hurt her
own, her only child, let all-embracing thoughts for all
that live be thine – and all-embracing love for all the
universe, in all its heights and depths and breadth,
unstinted love, unmarred by hate within, not rousing
enmity.[7]

Sutta-nipata

Gems
from the
Jewish Teachings

Behold, how good and how pleasant it is for brethren to dwell together in unity![8]

Psalms

Until the spirit be poured upon us from on high, And the wilderness become a fruitful field, And the fruitful field be counted for a forest. Then justice shall dwell in the wilderness, And righteousness shall abide in the fruitful field. And the work of righteousness shall be peace; And the effect of righteousness quietness and confidence for ever.[9]

Isaiah

Gems
from the
Christian Teachings

. . . Every kingdom divided against itself is brought to desolation; and every city or house divided against itself shall not stand.[10]

St Matthew

Let love be without dissimulation. Abhor that which is evil; cleave to that which is good. Be kindly affectioned one to another with brotherly love; in honour preferring one another; not slothful in business; fervent in spirit; serving the Lord; rejoicing in hope; patient in tribulation; continuing instant in prayer; distributing to the necessity of saints; given to hospitality. Bless them which persecute you: bless, and curse not. Rejoice with them that do rejoice, and weep with them that weep. Be of the same mind one toward another. Mind not high things, but condescend to men of low estate. Be not wise in your own conceits. Recompense to no man evil for evil. Provide things honest in the sight of all men. If it be possible, as much as lieth in you, live peaceably with all men.[11]

Romans

Gems
from the
Islamic Teachings

Moreover, to Moses gave we 'the Book', and we raised up apostles after him; and to Jesus, son of Mary, gave we clear proofs of his mission, and strengthened him by the Holy Spirit. So oft then as an apostle cometh to you with that which your souls desire not, swell ye with pride, and treat some as impostors, and slay others?[12]

Qur'án

Unto God belongeth the sovereignty of the Heavens
and of the Earth, and of all that they contain; and He
hath power over all things.[13]

Qur'án

Gems
from the
Bahá'í Teachings

'Consort with the followers of all religions in a spirit
of friendliness and fellowship.' Whatsoever hath led
the children of men to shun one another, and hath
caused dissensions and divisions amongst them, hath,
through the revelation of these words, been nullified
and abolished. From the heaven of God's Will, and for
the purpose of ennobling the world of being and of
elevating the minds and souls of men, hath been sent
down that which is the most effective instrument for the
education of the whole human race. The highest
essence and most perfect expression of whatsoever the
peoples of old have either said or written hath, through
this most potent Revelation, been sent down from the
heaven of the Will of the All-Possessing, the Ever-
Abiding God. Of old it hath been revealed: 'Love of
one's country is an element of the Faith of God.' The
Tongue of Grandeur hath, however, in the day of His
manifestation proclaimed: 'It is not his to boast who
loveth his country, but it is his who loveth the world.'[14]

Bahá'u'lláh

The bounties of the Blessed Perfection are infinite. We must endeavour to increase our capacity daily, to strengthen and enlarge our capabilities for receiving them, to become as perfect mirrors. The more polished and clean the mirror, the more effulgent is its reflection of the lights of the Sun of Truth. Be like a well-cultivated garden wherein the roses and variegated flowers of heaven are growing in fragrance and beauty. It is my hope that your hearts may become as ready ground, carefully tilled and prepared, upon which the divine showers of the bounties of the Blessed Perfection may descend and the zephyrs of this divine spring-time may blow with quickening breath. Then will the garden of your hearts bring forth its flowers of delightful fragrance to refresh the nostril of the heavenly Gardener. Let your hearts reflect the glories of the Sun of Truth in their many colours to gladden the eye of the divine Cultivator Who has nourished them. Day by day become more closely attracted in order that the love of God may illumine all those with whom you come in contact. Be as one spirit, one soul, leaves of one tree, flowers of one garden, waves of one ocean.

As difference in degree of capacity exists among human souls, as difference in capability is found, therefore, individualities will differ one from another. But in reality this is a reason for unity and not for discord and enmity. If the flowers of a garden were all of one colour, the effect would be monotonous to the eye; but if the colours are variegated, it is most pleasing and wonderful. The difference in adornment of colour and capacity of reflection among the flowers gives the garden its beauty and charm. Therefore, although we are of different individualities, different in ideas and of various fragrances, let us strive like flowers of the same divine garden to live together in harmony. Even though each soul has its own individual perfume and colour, all are reflecting the same light, all contributing fragrance to the same breeze which blows through the garden, all continuing to grow in complete harmony and accord. Become as waves of one sea, trees of one forest, growing in the utmost love, agreement and unity.[15]

'Abdu'l-Bahá

God has created us all human, and all countries of the world are parts of the same globe. We are all His servants. He is kind and just to all. Why should we be unkind and unjust to each other? He provides for all. Why should we deprive one another? He protects and preserves all. Why should we kill our fellow creatures? If this warfare and strife be for the sake of religion, it is evident that it violates the spirit and basis of all religion. All the divine Manifestations have proclaimed the oneness of God and the unity of mankind. They have taught that men should love and mutually help each other in order that they might progress. Now if this conception of religion be true, its essential principle is the oneness of humanity. The fundamental truth of the Manifestations is peace. This underlies all religion, all justice. The divine purpose is that men should live in unity, concord and agreement and should love one another. Consider the virtues of the human world and realize that the oneness of humanity is the primary foundation of them all. Read the Gospel and the other Holy Books. You will find their fundamentals are one and the same. Therefore, unity is the essential

truth of religion and, when so understood, embraces all
the virtues of the human world. Praise be to God! This
knowledge has been spread, eyes have been opened,
and ears have become attentive. Therefore, we must
endeavour to promulgate and practise the religion of
God which has been founded by all the Prophets. And
the religion of God is absolute love and unity.[16]

'Abdu'l-Bahá

Love

Love is the most powerful force in the universe. If we
reflect on the qualities we admire in other people, their
ability to express love to others is one of the most
important. Love is a basic teaching of all the religions.
The Prophets of God tell us about the different kinds of
love and about the importance of love. Love can keep
people and nations in harmony with each other. Love
unites families and has the power to unite the world.

Songs, poems, plays and novels have been written
about love. The qualities of love such as kindness,
patience, caring, remembering, tenderness, purity of
motive, selflessness, compassion, courtesy, consider-
ation, forgiveness, generosity, assistance and servitude
are brought into clear focus when they are compared
with the opposite qualities of the ego and human
selfishness. The sacred writings of the religions provide
guidance and inspiration to help us develop these
attributes of love within ourselves. Perhaps this is one
of the most important things we can learn during our
lives. As we grow spiritually we begin to reflect the
attributes of love to others.

We are familiar with many physical laws of the
universe; as we study and develop we become more
aware of the spiritual laws. We are told in the sacred
verses of the religions that love is the highest law in the
universe, which shows how important love is in the
whole pattern of creation. We should strive to make

love the dominating principle in our individual lives. The lives of the Prophets of God demonstrate the kinds of love that we most admire. By studying the stories of their lives and their teachings we will come to understand the importance of developing the qualities of love in our individual lives.

The sacred writings of the religions encourage us to expand our concepts of love from the love we have for our dear ones to a love for all humanity, regardless of the differences of cultural background or physical appearance. A unified world must be built on the foundation of love; and this foundation can be constructed by connecting, one by one, all the people in the world with the golden threads of love.

Gems
from the
Hindu Teachings

Let a man feel hatred for no contingent being,
Let him be friendly, compassionate,
Let him be done with thoughts of 'I' and 'mine',
The same in pleasure as in pain, long-suffering,

Content and ever integrated,
His self restrained, his purpose firm,
Let him mind and soul (buddhi) be steeped in Me,
Let him worship Me with love (bhakta):
Then will I love him (in return).

That man I love from whom the people do not
   shrink,
And who does not shrink from them,
Who's free from exaltation, fear,
Impatience and excitement.

I love the man who has no expectation,
Is pure and skilled, indifferent,
Who has no worries, and gives up
All (selfish) enterprise, wrapt up in (bhakta) Me.

I love the man who hates not, nor exults,
Who mourns not nor desires,
Who puts away both pleasant and unpleasant things,
Who's loyal, devoted and devout (bhaktimat).

I love the man who is the same
To friend and foe, (the same)
Whether he be respected or despised,
The same in heat and cold, in pleasure as in pain
   . . . [1]

Bhagavad-Gita

Gems
from the
Buddhist Teachings

We are what we think,
having become what we thought,

Like the wheel that follows the cart-pulling ox,
Sorrow follows an evil thought.

And joy follows a pure thought,
like a shadow faithfully tailing a man.
We are what we think,
having become what we thought.

How will hate leave him if a man forever thinks,
'He abused me, he hit me, he defeated me, he
    robbed me'?

Will hate ever touch him if he does not think,
'He abused me, he hit me, he defeated me, he
    robbed me'?

There is only one eternal law:
Hate never destroys hate; only love does.[2]

Dhammapada

If creatures should know
(Just as the Great Sage hath said),
What wondrous fruit
Cometh from giving gifts.

Having with undisturbed mind
Put away all stain of selfishness
They would give proper gifts to the deserving;
From this act there cometh (to them) great reward.

And having given much food
As a gift to the deserving,

Benefactors, when they leave
This human life (manussatta), do go to heaven.

And those that have gone to heaven
Rejoice there in bliss;
(And) losing their selfishness, they enjoy
The result of generosity.[3]

Buddha

Conquer anger by love . . .[4]

Dhammapada

Ah, happily do we live without hate among the hateful;
amidst hateful men we dwell unhating.[5]

Dhammapada

Gems
from the
Jewish Teachings

. . . in that I command thee this day to love the Lord
thy God, to walk in His ways, and to keep His
commandments and His statutes and His ordinances;
then thou shalt live and multiply, and the Lord thy God
shall bless thee in the land whither thou goest in to
possess it.[6]

Deuteronomy

Hear, O Israel: the Lord our God, the Lord is one.
And thou shalt love the Lord thy God with all thy
heart, and with all thy soul, and with all thy might. And
these words, which I command thee this day, shall be
upon thy heart; and thou shalt teach them diligently
unto thy children, and shalt talk of them when thou sittest
in thy house, and when thou walkest by the way, and
when thou liest down, and when thou risest up.[7]

Deuteronomy

I love them that love me, And those that seek me
earnestly shall find me. Riches and honour are with me;
Yea, enduring riches and righteousness. My fruit is
better than gold, yea, than fine gold; And my produce
than choice silver. I walk in the way of righteousness,
In the midst of the paths of justice; That I may cause
those that love me to inherit substance, And that I may
fill their treasuries.[8]

Proverbs

Gems
from the
Christian Teachings

Jesus said unto him, Thou shalt love the Lord thy God
with all thy heart, and with all thy soul, and with all thy
mind. This is the first and great commandment. And
the second is like unto it, Thou shalt love thy neighbour

as thyself. On these two commandments hang all the
law and the prophets.[9]

St Matthew

For God so loved the world, that he gave his only
begotten Son, that whosoever believeth in him should
not perish, but have everlasting life.[10]

St John

Though I speak with the tongues of men and of angels,
and have not charity, I am become as sounding brass,
or a tinkling cymbal. And though I have the gift of
prophecy, and understand all mysteries, and all knowledge; and though I have all faith, so that I could
remove mountains, and have not charity, I am nothing.
And though I bestow all my goods to feed the poor, and
though I give my body to be burned, and have not
charity, it profiteth me nothing. Charity suffereth long,
and is kind; charity envieth not; charity vaunteth not
itself, is not puffed up, doth not behave itself unseemly,
seeketh not her own, is not easily provoked, thinketh
no evil; rejoiceth not in iniquity, but rejoiceth in the
truth; beareth all things, believeth all things, hopeth all
things, endureth all things. Charity never faileth: but
whether there be prophecies, they shall fail; whether
there be tongues, they shall cease; whether there be
knowledge, it shall vanish away. For we know in part,
and we prophesy in part. But when that which is perfect
is come, then that which is in part shall be done away.
When I was a child, I spake as a child, I understood as a
child, I thought as a child: but when I became a man, I

put away childish things. For now we see through a
glass, darkly; but then face to face: now I know in part;
but then shall I know even as also I am known. And
now abideth faith, hope, charity, these three; but the
greatest of these is charity.[11]

I Corinthians

Beloved, let us love one another: for love is of God;
and every one that loveth is born of God, and knoweth
God. He that loveth not knoweth not God; for God is
love.[12]

I John

No man hath seen God at any time. If we love one
another, God dwelleth in us, and his love is perfected in
us.[13]

I John

As the Father hath loved me, so have I loved you:
continue ye in my love. If ye keep my commandments,
ye shall abide in my love; even as I have kept my
Father's commandments, and abide in his love. These
things have I spoken unto you, that my joy might
remain in you, and that your joy might be full. This is
my commandment, That ye love one another, as I have
loved you. Greater love hath no man than this, that a
man lay down his life for his friends.[14]

St John

And we have known and believed the love that God hath to us. God is love; and he that dwelleth in love dwelleth in God, and God in him.[15]

I John

But as it is written, Eye hath not seen, nor ear heard, neither have entered into the heart of man, the things which God hath prepared for them that love him. But God hath revealed them unto us by his Spirit: for the Spirit searcheth all things, yea, the deep things of God. For what man knoweth the things of a man, save the spirit of man which is in him? even so the things of God knoweth no man, but the Spirit of God. Now we have received, not the spirit of the world, but the spirit which is of God; that we might know the things that are freely given to us of God.[16]

I Corinthians

Gems
from the
Islamic Teachings

But love will the God of Mercy vouchsafe to those who believe and do the things that be right.[17]

Qur'án

Thy Lord hath ordained that ye worship none but him; and, kindness to your parents, whether one or both of

them attain old age with thee: and say not to them 'Fie!'
neither reproach them; but speak to them both with
respectful speech; and defer humbly to them out of
tenderness; and say, 'Lord have compassion on them
both, even as they reared me when I was little.'

Your Lord well knoweth what is in your souls; he
knoweth whether ye be righteous.[18]

Qur'án

This is what God announceth to his servants who
believe and do the things that are right. SAY: For this
ask I no wage of you, save the love of my kin. And
whoever shall have won the merit of a good deed, we
will increase good to him therewith; for God is forgiving,
grateful.[19]

Qur'án

Gems
from the
Bahá'í Teachings

What a power is love! It is the most wonderful, the
greatest of all living powers.

Love gives life to the lifeless. Love lights a flame in
the heart that is cold. Love brings hope to the hopeless
and gladdens the hearts of the sorrowful.

In the world of existence there is indeed no greater
power than the power of love. When the heart of man is

aglow with the flame of love, he is ready to sacrifice all – even his life. In the Gospel it is said God is love.

There are four kinds of love. The first is the love that flows from God to man; it consists of the inexhaustible graces, the Divine effulgence and heavenly illumination. Through this love the world of being receives life. Through this love man is endowed with physical existence, until, through the breath of the Holy Spirit – this same love – he receives eternal life and becomes the image of the Living God. This love is the origin of all the love in the world of creation.

The second is the love that flows from man to God. This is faith, attraction to the Divine, enkindlement, progress, entrance into the Kingdom of God, receiving the Bounties of God, illumination with the lights of the Kingdom. This love is the origin of all philanthropy; this love causes the hearts of men to reflect the rays of the Sun of Reality.

The third is the love of God towards the Self or Identity of God. This is the transfiguration of His Beauty, the reflection of Himself in the mirror of His Creation. This is the reality of love, the Ancient Love, the Eternal Love. Through one ray of this Love all other love exists.

The fourth is the love of man for man. The love which exists between the hearts of believers is prompted by the ideal of the unity of spirits. This love is attained through the knowledge of God, so that men see the Divine Love reflected in the heart. Each sees in the other the Beauty of God reflected in the soul, and finding this point of similarity, they are attracted to one another in love. This love will make all men the waves of one sea, this love will make them all the stars of one heaven and the fruits of one tree. This love will bring the realization of true accord, the foundation of real unity.

But the love which sometimes exists between friends is not (true) love, because it is subject to transmutation; this is merely fascination. As the breeze blows, the slender trees yield. If the wind is in the East the tree leans to the West, and if the wind turns to the West the tree leans to the East. This kind of love is originated by the accidental conditions of life. This is not love, it is merely acquaintanceship; it is subject to change.

Today you will see two souls apparently in close friendship; tomorrow all this may be changed. Yesterday they were ready to die for one another, today they shun one another's society! This is not love; it is the yielding of the hearts to the accidents of life. When that which has caused this 'love' to exist passes, the love passes also; this is not in reality love.

Love is only of the four kinds that I have explained. (a) The love of God towards the identity of God. Christ has said God is Love. (b) The love of God for His children – for His servants. (c) The love of man for God and (d) the love of man for man. These four kinds of love originate from God. These are rays from the Sun of Reality; these are the Breathings of the Holy Spirit; these are the Signs of the Reality.[20]

'Abdu'l-Bahá

Love is the most great Law that ruleth this mighty and heavenly cycle, the unique power that bindeth together

the divers elements of this material world, the supreme
magnetic force that directeth the movements of the
spheres in the celestial realms. Love revealeth with
unfailing and limitless power the mysteries latent in the
universe.[21]

'Abdu'l-Bahá

Therefore, we must not make distinctions between
individual members of the human family. We must not
consider any soul as barren or deprived. Our duty lies
in educating souls so that the Sun of the bestowals of
God shall become resplendent in them, and this is
possible through the power of the oneness of humanity.
The more love is expressed among mankind and the
stronger the power of unity, the greater will be this
reflection and revelation, for the greatest bestowal of
God is love. Love is the source of all the bestowals of
God. Until love takes possession of the heart no other
divine bounty can be revealed in it.

All the prophets have striven to make love manifest
in the hearts of men. His Holiness Jesus Christ sought
to create this love in the hearts. He suffered all
difficulties and ordeals that perchance the human heart
might become the fountain source of love. Therefore,
we must strive with all our heart and soul that this love
may take possession of us so that all humanity –
whether it be in the East or in the West – may be
connected through the bond of this divine affection; for
we are all the waves of one sea; we have come into
being through the same bestowal and are recipients
from the same centre. The lights of earth are all

acceptable, but the centre of effulgence is the sun, and
we must direct our gaze to the sun. God is the Supreme
Centre. The more we turn toward this Centre of Light,
the greater will be our capacity.[22]

'Abdu'l-Bahá

Ye must become brilliant lamps. Ye must shine as stars
radiating the light of love toward all mankind. May you
be the cause of love amongst the nations . . . Make
peace with all the world. Love everybody; serve everybody. All are the servants of God. God has created all.
He provideth for all. He is kind to all. Therefore, must
we be kind to all.[23]

'Abdu'l-Bahá

With hearts set aglow by the fire of the love of God and
spirits refreshed by the food of the heavenly spirit you
must go forth as the disciples nineteen hundred years
ago, quickening the hearts of men by the call of glad
tidings, the light of God in your faces, severed from
everything save God. Therefore, order your lives
in accordance with the first principle of the divine
teaching, which is love. Service to humanity is service to God. Let the love and light of the Kingdom radiate through you until all who look upon
you shall be illumined by its reflection. Be as stars,
brilliant and sparkling in the loftiness of their heavenly
station.[24]

'Abdu'l-Bahá

The advent of the prophets and the revelation of the Holy Books is intended to create love between souls and friendship between the inhabitants of the earth. Real love is impossible unless one turn his face towards God and be attracted to His Beauty.[25]

'Abdu'l-Bahá

Guidance

Personal guidance is of the utmost importance to each of us. All of us want to live meaningful lives, to have peaceful minds, to be happy, to stop needless worrying, and to develop habits of thinking in positive ways. We would like to be able to solve our problems, to be healthy, to develop friendships, to become well-educated, to achieve, to draw on spiritual power in our lives, and to learn to love ourselves and other people.

Where can we find assistance and knowledge to help us achieve these goals? One of the important purposes of religion is to provide inspiration and guidance for humankind. Thousands of years of guidance recorded in the sacred writings of the world's religions provide an excellent source of material to help us achieve many of the goals mentioned above. We need to search everywhere for answers. Education should be extremely important to us. We must continually search for guidance and we cannot expect to have most of our problems solved by others. The guidance in the sacred writings must be sought out, read, studied, meditated upon, and sometimes memorized to provide the assistance which we seek.

The following selections provide inspiration and guidance on a number of subjects not included in previous chapters. They represent only a small part of the vast range of subjects addressed in the sacred writings and teachings of these religions.

Gems
from the
Hindu Teachings

The Blessed Lord said:
Attach thy mind to Me:
Engaged in Yogic exercise, put thy trust in Me:
(This doing) listen how thou mayest come to know
  Me
In my entirety, all doubt dispelled.

This wisdom derived from sacred writ
And the wisdom of experience
I shall proclaim to thee, leaving nothing unsaid.
This knowing, never again will any other thing
That needs to be known remain.

Among thousands of men but one, maybe,
Will strive for self-perfection;
And even among these (athletes) who have won
  perfection('s crown)
But one, maybe, will come to know Me as I really
  am.

Eightfold divided is my Nature – thus:
Earth, water, fire and air,
Space, mind, and also soul (buddhi),
The ego (last).

This is the lower: but other than this
I have a higher Nature; this too must thou know.

(And this is) Nature seen as life
By which this universe (jagat) is kept in being.

From these (two Natures) all beings take their origin;
Be very sure of this.
Of the whole (wide) universe
The origin and the dissolution too am I.

Higher than I
There's nothing whatsoever:
On Me the universe (sarvam) is strung
Like clustered pearls upon a thread.

In water I am the flavour,
In sun and moon the light,
In all the Vedas Om (the sacred syllable),
In space I'm sound: in man (his) manliness am I.

Pure fragrance in the earth am I,
Flame's onset in the fire;
(And) life (am I) in all contingent beings,
In ascetics (their) fierce austerity.

Know that I am the eternal seed
Of all contingent beings:
Reason in the rational,
Glory in the glorious am I.

Power in the powerful I –
(Such power) as knows nor passion nor desire:
Desire am I in contingent beings,
(But such desire as is) not at war with right
    (dharma).

Know too that all states of being, whether they be
Of (Nature's constituent) Goodness, Passion or
   Darkness,
Proceed from Me;
But I am not in them, they are in Me.

By these three states of being
Inhering in the 'constituents'
This whole universe is led astray,
And does not understand
That I am far beyond them:
I neither change nor pass away.[1]

                                        Bhagavad-Gita

And so, detached, perform unceasingly
The works that must be done
For the man detached who labours on (karma),
To the Highest must win through.

For only by working on (karma) did Janaka
And his like attain perfection.
Or if again for the welfare of the world thou carest,
Then shouldst thou work (and act).

(For) whatever the noblest does,
That too will others do:
The standard that he sets
All the world will follow.

In the three worlds there's nothing
That I must do at all,
Nor anything unattained which I have not attained;
Yet work (is the element) in which I move.

For were I not tirelessly
To busy myself with works,
Then would men everywhere
Follow in my footsteps.

If I were not to do my work,
These worlds would fall to ruin,
And I should be a worker of confusion,
Destroying these (my) creatures.

As witless (fools) perform their works
Attached to the work (they do).
So, unattached, should the wise man do,
Longing to bring about the welfare of the world.

Let not the wise man split the mind (buddhi)
Of witless men attached to work:
Let him encourage all (manner of) works,
(Himself,) though busy, controlled and integrated
   (yukta).[2]

Bhagavad-Gita

Let a man, remaining in this world.
And before he is released from the body('s bondage)
Stand fast against the onset of anger and desire;
Only so in joy will he be integrated.

His joy within, his bliss within,
His light within, that Yogin
Becomes Brahman and draws nigh
To Nirvana that is Brahman too.[3]

Bhagavad-Gita

Know this:
The self is the owner of the chariot,
The chariot is the body,
Soul (buddhi) is the (body's) charioteer,
Mind the reins (that curb it).

Senses, they say, are the (chariot's) steeds,
Their objects the tract before them:
What, then, is the subject of experience?
'Self, sense and mind conjoined,' wise men reply.

Who knows not how to discriminate (avijnanavat)
With mind undisciplined (a-yukta) the while, –
Like vicious steeds untamed, his senses
He cannot master – he their charioteer.

But he who does know how to discriminate
With mind (controlled and) disciplined, –
Like well-trained steeds, his senses
He masters (fully) – he their charioteer.[4]

Katha Upanishad

Gems
from the
Buddhist Teachings

Choose friends, virtuous and excellent.
Shun the low-minded and ill-doing.

To drink Dhamma is to be serene.
Wisdom finds delight in the noble Dhamma.

Planners make canals,
archers shoot arrows,
craftsmen fashion woodwork,
the wise man moulds himself.

Wind will not move rock,
nor praise and blame a wise man.

The words of the Dhamma flow into him:
he is clear and peaceful like a lake.

Good men do not stop working.
Good men do not gossip, good men are
   undemanding.
Joy does not affect them, nor sorrow.
Good men are constant.[5]

Dhammapada

Desire begetteth unseemliness (anattha);
Desire exciteth the thoughts;
A person is not aware of this danger
Which is born from within.

The man that is dominated by Desire
Doth not know what is seemly and seeth not the
   Law;

That man whom Desire doth accompany,
Becometh like unto murky (andha) darkness.

And he that hath abandoned Desire,
And desireth not the things that make for Desire –
From him Desire doth pass away
As doth a drop of water from the lotus.

Hate begetteth unseemliness;
Hate exciteth the thoughts;
A person is not aware of this danger
Which is born from within.

The man that is dominated by Anger
Doth not know what is seemly and seeth not the
   Law;
That man whom Hate doth accompany,
Becometh like unto murky darkness.

And he that hath abandoned Hate,
And hateth not the things that make for Hate –
From Him Hate doth pass away
As doth Tal fruit from its stem.

Delusion begetteth unseemliness;
Delusion exciteth the thoughts;
A person is not aware of this danger
Which is born from within.

The man that is under Delusion
Doth not know what is seemly and seeth not the
   Law;

That man whom Delusion doth accompany
Becometh like unto murky darkness.

And he that hath abandoned Delusion, and is not
    deluded
By the things which make for Delusion –
He doth dispel all Delusion,
As the rising sun (dispelleth) the darkness.[6]

Buddha

Value your self, look after your self.
Be watchful throughout your life.

Learn what is right; test it and see;
then teach others – is the way of the pandit.

You are your own refuge;
there is no other refuge.
This refuge is hard to achieve.

One's self is the lord of oneself;
there is no other lord.
This lord is difficult to conquer.

Diamond breaks diamond,
evil crushes the evildoer.

As the creeper strangles the sal tree,
evil overpowers the evildoer.
His enemy could not be more delighted.

Easy to do an evil deed,
easy to harm oneself.
Difficult to do a good deed,
very difficult indeed.

Like the khattaka tree, dead after fruit-bearing,
or cut down for the sake of its fruit,
the foolish man sows his own destruction
by mocking the wise, the noble, and the virtuous.

You cannot save another, you can only save yourself.
You do the evil deed, you reap the bitter fruit.
You leave it undone, your self is purified.

Better is your own Dhamma, however weak,
than the Dhamma of another, however noble.
Look after your self, and be firm in your goal.[7]

Dhammapada

Gems
from the
Jewish Teachings

Thou wilt guide me with Thy counsel, And afterward receive me with glory. Whom have I in heaven but Thee? And beside Thee I desire none upon earth. My flesh and my heart faileth; But God is the rock of my heart and my portion for ever.[8]

Psalms

Hast thou not known? hast thou not heard that the everlasting God, the Lord, The creator of the ends of the earth, Fainteth not, neither is weary? His discernment is past searching out. He giveth power to the faint; And to him that hath no might He increaseth strength. Even the youths shall faint and be weary, And the young men shall utterly fall; But they that wait for the Lord shall renew their strength; They shall mount up with wings as eagles; They shall run, and not be weary; They shall walk, and not faint.[9]

Isaiah

Happy is the man that findeth wisdom, and the man that obtaineth understanding. For the merchandise of it is better than the merchandise of silver, And the gain thereof than fine gold. She is more precious than rubies; And all the things thou canst desire are not to be compared unto her. Length of days is in her right hand; In her left hand are riches and honour. Her ways are ways of pleasantness, And all her paths are peace. She is a tree of life to them that lay hold upon her, And happy is every one that holdeth her fast. The Lord by wisdom founded the earth; By understanding He established the heavens. By His knowledge the depths were broken up, And the skies drop down the dew. My son, let not them depart from thine eyes; Keep sound wisdom and discretion; So shall they be life unto thy soul, And grace to thy neck. Then shalt thou walk in thy way securely, And thou shalt not dash thy foot. When thou liest down, thou shalt not be afraid; Yea, thou shalt lie down, and thy sleep shall be sweet.[10]

Proverbs

Gems
from the
Christian Teachings

. . . It is written, Man shall not live by bread alone, but by every word that proceedeth out of the mouth of God.[11]

St Matthew

Honour thy father and thy mother: and, Thou shalt love thy neighbour as thyself.[12]

St Matthew

Heaven and earth shall pass away, but my words shall not pass away.[13]

St Matthew

For if a man think himself to be something, when he is nothing, he deceiveth himself. But let every man prove his own work, and then shall he have rejoicing in himself alone, and not in another. For every man shall bear his own burden. Let him that is taught in the word communicate unto him that teacheth in all good things. Be not deceived; God is not mocked: for whatsoever a man soweth, that shall he also reap.[14]

Galatians

The same day went Jesus out of the house, and sat by the sea side. And great multitudes were gathered together unto him, so that he went into a ship, and sat; and the whole multitude stood on the shore. And he spake many things unto them in parables, saying, Behold, a sower went forth to sow; and when he sowed, some seeds fell by the way side, and the fowls came and devoured them up: Some fell upon stony places, where they had not much earth: and forthwith they sprung up, because they had no deepness of earth: And when the sun was up, they were scorched; and because they had no root, they withered away. And some fell among thorns; and the thorns sprung up, and choked them: But other fell into good ground, and brought forth fruit, some an hundredfold, some sixtyfold, some thirtyfold. Who hath ears to hear, let him hear.[15]

St Matthew

And he said, A certain man had two sons: and the younger of them said to his father, Father, give me the portion of goods that falleth to me. And he divided unto them his living. And not many days after the younger son gathered all together, and took his journey into a far country, and there wasted his substance with riotous living. And when he had spent all, there arose a mighty famine in that land; and he began to be in want. And he went and joined himself to a citizen of that country and he sent him into his fields to feed swine. And he would fain have filled his belly with the husks that the swine did eat: and no man gave unto him. And when he came to himself, he said, How many hired servants of my father's have bread enough and to spare, and I perish with hunger! I will arise and go to my father, and will say unto him, Father, I have sinned against heaven, and before thee, and am no more worthy to be called thy son: make me as one of thy hired servants. And he arose, and came to his father. But when he was yet a great way off, his father saw him, and had compassion, and ran, and fell on his neck, and kissed him. And the son said unto him, Father, I have sinned against heaven, and in thy sight, and am no more worthy to be called thy son. But the father said to his servants, Bring forth the best robe, and put it on him; and put a ring on his hand, and shoes on his feet: and bring hither the fatted calf, and kill it; and let us eat, and be merry: for this my son was dead, and is alive again; he was lost, and is found. And they began to be merry. Now his elder son was in the field: and as he came and drew nigh to the house, he heard musick and dancing. And he called one of the servants, and asked what these things meant. And he said unto him, Thy brother is come; and thy father hath killed the fatted calf, because he hath received him safe and sound. And he was angry, and would not go in: therefore came his father out, and entreated him. And he answering said to his father, Lo, these many years do I serve thee, neither transgressed I at any time thy commandment: and yet thou never gavest me a kid, that I might make merry with my friends: but as soon as this thy son was come, which hath devoured thy living with harlots, thou hast killed for him the fatted calf. And he said unto him, Son, thou art ever with me, and all that I have is thine. It was meet that we should make merry, and be glad: for this thy brother was dead, and is alive again; and was lost, and is found.[16]

St Luke

Stand therefore, having your loins girt about with truth, and having on the breastplate of righteousness; and your feet shod with the preparation of the gospel of peace; above all, taking the shield of faith, wherewith ye shall be able to quench all the fiery darts of the wicked. And take the helmet of salvation, and the sword of the Spirit, which is the word of God.[17]

Ephesians

But love ye your enemies, and do good, and lend, hoping for nothing again; and your reward shall be great, and ye shall be the children of the Highest: for he is kind unto the unthankful and to the evil. Be ye therefore merciful, as your Father also is merciful. Judge not, and ye shall not be judged: condemn not, and ye shall not be condemned: forgive and ye shall be forgiven: give, and it shall be given unto you; good measure, pressed down, and shaken together, and running over, shall men give into your bosom. For with the same measure that ye mete withal it shall be measured to you again.[18]

St Luke

Children, obey your parents in the Lord: for this is right. Honour thy father and mother; which is the first commandment with promise; that it may be well with thee, and thou mayest live long on the earth. And, ye fathers, provoke not your children to wrath: but bring them up in the nurture and admonition of the Lord.[19]

Ephesians

I have shewed you all things, how that so labouring ye
ought to support the weak, and to remember the words
of the Lord Jesus, how he said, It is more blessed to
give than to receive.[20]

Acts

There is no fear in love; but perfect love casteth out
fear: because fear hath torment. He that feareth is not
made perfect in love. We love him, because he first
loved us. If a man say, I love God, and hateth his
brother, he is a liar: for he that loveth not his brother
whom he hath seen, how can he love God whom he
hath not seen? And this commandment have we from
him, That he who loveth God love his brother also.[21]

I John

Husbands, love your wives, even as Christ also loved
the church, and gave himself for it; that he might
sanctify and cleanse it with the washing of water by the
word, that he might present it to himself a glorious
church, not having spot, or wrinkle, or any such thing;
but that it should be holy and without blemish. So
ought men to love their wives as their own bodies. He
that loveth his wife loveth himself. For no man ever yet
hated his own flesh; but nourisheth and cherisheth it,
even as the Lord the church: for we are members of his
body, of his flesh, and of his bones. For this cause shall
a man leave his father and mother, and shall be joined
unto his wife, and they two shall be one flesh. This is a
great mystery: but I speak concerning Christ and the
church. Nevertheless let every one of you in particular

so love his wife even as himself; and the wife see that
she reverence her husband.[22]

Ephesians

Gems
from the
Islamic Teachings

For truth hath he created the Heavens and the Earth: It
is of Him that the night returneth upon the day and that
the day returneth upon the night: and He controlleth
the sun and the moon so that each speedeth to an
appointed goal. Is He not the Mighty, the Gracious?

He created you all of one man, from whom He
afterwards formed his wife; and of cattle He hath sent
down to you four pairs. In the wombs of your mothers
did He create you by creation upon creation in triple
darkness. It is He who is God your Lord: the kingdom
is His: There is no God but He. How then are ye so
turned aside from Him?

Suppose ye render him no thanks! yet forsooth is
God rich without you: but He is not pleased with
thanklessness in His servants: yet if ye be thankful He
will be pleased with you. The soul burdened with its
own works shall not be burdened with the burden of
another: hereafter shall ye return to your Lord, and he
will tell you of all your works,

For he knoweth the very secrets of your breasts.[23]

Qur'án

If all the trees that are upon the earth were to become pens, and if God should after that swell the sea into seven seas of ink, His words would not be exhausted: for God is Mighty, Wise.

Your creation and your quickening hereafter, are but as those of a single individual. Verily, God Heareth, Seeth!

Seest thou not that God causeth the night to come in upon the day, and the day to come in upon the night? and that he hath subjected the sun and the moon to laws by which each speedeth along to an appointed goal? and that God therefore is acquainted with that which ye do?

This, for that God is the truth; and that whatever ye call upon beside Him is a vain thing; and that God – He is the High, the Great.

Seest thou not how the ships speed on in the sea, through the favour of God, that he may shew you of his signs? for herein are signs to all patient, grateful ones.

When the waves cover them like dark shadows they call upon God as with sincere religion; but when He safely landeth them, some of them there are who halt between two opinions. Yet none reject our signs but all deceitful, ungrateful ones.

O men! fear ye your Lord, and dread the day whereon father shall not atone for son, neither shall a son in the least atone for his father.

Aye! the promise of God is a truth. Let not this present life then deceive you concerning God.

Aye! God! – with Him is the knowledge of the Hour: and He sendeth down the rain – and He knoweth what is in the wombs – but no soul knoweth what it shall have gotten on the morrow: neither knoweth any soul in what land it shall die. But God is knowing, informed of all.[24]

Qur'án

Assuredly they who say, 'Our Lord is God,' and take the straight way to Him – no fear shall come on them, neither shall they be put to grief:

These shall be the inmates of Paradise to remain therein for ever – the recompense of their deeds!

Moreover, we have enjoined on man to shew kindness to his parents. With pain his mother beareth him; with pain she bringeth him forth: and his bearing and his weaning is thirty months; until when he attaineth his strength, and attaineth to forty years, he saith, 'O my Lord! stir me up to be grateful for thy favours wherewith thou hast favoured me and my parents, and to do good works which shall please thee: and prosper me in my offspring: for to thee am I turned, and am resigned to thy will' (am a Muslim).

These are they from whom we will accept their best works, and whose evil works we will pass by; among the inmates shall they be of Paradise – a true promise which they are promised.

But he who saith to his parents, 'Fie on you both! Promise ye me that I shall be taken forth from the grave alive, when whole generations have already passed away before me?' But they both will implore the help of God, and say, 'Alas for thee! Believe: for the promise of God is true.' But he saith, 'It is no more than a fable of the ancients.'

These are they in whom the sentence passed on the nations, djinn and men, who flourished before them, is made good. They shall surely perish.

And there are grades for all, according to their works, that God may repay them for their works; and they shall not be dealt with unfairly.[25]

Qur'án

Thou truly canst not guide whom thou desirest; but God guideth whom He will; and He best knoweth those who yield to guidance.[26]

Qur'án

God is the Light of the Heavens and of the Earth. His Light is like a niche in which is a lamp – the lamp encased in glass – the glass, as it were, a glistening star. From a blessed tree is it lighted, the olive neither of the East nor of the West, whose oil would well nigh shine out, even though fire touched it not! It is light upon light. God guideth whom He will to His light, and God setteth forth parables to men, for God knoweth all things.[27]

Qur'án

No doubt is there about this Book: It is a guidance to the God-fearing,

Who believe in the unseen, who observe prayer, and out of what we have bestowed on them, expend for God;

And who believe in what hath been sent down to thee, and in what hath been sent down before thee, and full faith have they in the life to come:

These are guided by their Lord; and with these it shall be well.[28]

Qur'án

And whoso maketh efforts for us, in our ways will we guide them: for God is assuredly with those who do righteous deeds.[29]

Qur'án

And truly thy Lord will repay every one according to their works! for He is well aware of what they do.[30]

Qur'án

Gems
from the
Bahá'í Teachings

And yet, is not the object of every Revelation to effect a transformation in the whole character of mankind, a transformation that shall manifest itself both outwardly and inwardly, that shall affect both its inner life and external conditions? For if the character of mankind be not changed, the futility of God's universal Manifestations would be apparent.[31]

Bahá'u'lláh

The source of all learning is the knowledge of God, exalted be His Glory, and this cannot be attained save through the knowledge of His Divine Manifestation.[32]

Bahá'u'lláh

A good character is, verily, the best mantle for men from God. With it He adorneth the temples of His loved ones. By My life! The light of a good character surpasseth the light of the sun and the radiance thereof. Whoso attaineth unto it is accounted as a jewel among men. The glory and upliftment of the world must needs depend upon it.[33]

Bahá'u'lláh

If any man were to meditate on that which the Scriptures, sent down from the heaven of God's holy Will, have revealed, he would readily recognize that their purpose is that all men shall be regarded as one soul . . . If the learned and worldly-wise men of this age were to allow mankind to inhale the fragrance of fellowship and love, every understanding heart would apprehend the meaning of true liberty, and discover the secret of undisturbed peace and absolute composure.[34]

Bahá'u'lláh

That one indeed is a man who, today, dedicateth himself to the service of the entire human race. The Great Being saith: Blessed and happy is he that ariseth to promote the best interests of the peoples and kindreds of the earth. In another passage He hath

proclaimed: It is not for him to pride himself who
loveth his own country, but rather for him who loveth
the whole world. The earth is but one country, and
mankind its citizens.[35]

Bahá'u'lláh

God loveth those who are pure. Naught in the Bayán
and in the sight of God is more loved than purity and
immaculate cleanliness . . .

   God desireth not to see, in the Dispensation of the
Bayán, any soul deprived of joy and radiance. He
indeed desireth that under all conditions, all may be
adorned with such purity, both inwardly and
outwardly, that no repugnance may be caused even to
themselves, how much less unto others.[36]

The Báb

If love and agreement are manifest in a single family,
that family will advance, become illumined and spiritual; but if enmity and hatred exist within it, destruction and dispersion are inevitable. This is, likewise,
true of a city. If those who dwell within it manifest a
spirit of accord and fellowship, it will progress steadily
and human conditions become brighter, whereas
through enmity and strife it will be degraded and its
inhabitants scattered. In the same way, the people of a
nation develop and advance toward civilization and
enlightenment through love and accord and are dis-
integrated by war and strife. Finally, this is true of
humanity itself in the aggregate. When love is realized
and the ideal spiritual bonds unite the hearts of men,

the whole human race will be uplifted, the world will continually grow more spiritual and radiant and the happiness and tranquillity of mankind be immeasurably increased. Warfare and strife will be uprooted, disagreement and dissension pass away and universal peace unite the nations and peoples of the world. All mankind will dwell together as one family, blend as the waves of one sea, shine as stars of one firmament and appear as fruits of the same tree. This is the happiness and felicity of humankind. This is the illumination of man, the eternal glory and everlasting life; this is the divine bestowal.[37]

'Abdu'l-Bahá

. . . among the teachings of Bahá'u'lláh is that religious, racial, political, economic and patriotic prejudices destroy the edifice of humanity. As long as these prejudices prevail, the world of humanity will not have rest. For a period of 6,000 years history informs us about the world of humanity. During these 6,000 years the world of humanity has not been free from war, strife, murder and bloodthirstiness. In every period war has been waged in one country or another and that war was due to either religious prejudice, racial prejudice, political prejudice or patriotic prejudice. It has therefore been ascertained and proved that all prejudices are destructive of the human edifice. As long as these prejudices persist, the struggle for existence must remain dominant, and bloodthirstiness and rapacity continue. Therefore, even as was the case in the past, the world of humanity cannot be saved from the darkness of nature and cannot attain illumination

except through the abandonment of prejudices and the
acquisition of the morals of the Kingdom.[38]

'Abdu'l-Bahá

Through education the ignorant become learned, the
cowardly become valiant. Through cultivation the
crooked branch becomes straight; the acid, bitter fruit
of the mountains and woods becomes sweet and deli-
cious; and the five-petalled flower becomes hundred
petalled. Through education savage nations become
civilized, and even the animals become domesticated.
Education must be considered as most important, for as
diseases in the world of bodies are extremely contagious, so, in the same way, qualities of spirit and
heart are extremely contagious. Education has a
universal influence, and the differences caused by it are
very great.

Perhaps someone will say that, since the capacity and
worthiness of men differ, therefore, the difference of
capacity certainly causes the difference of characters.

But this is not so, for capacity is of two kinds: natural
capacity and acquired capacity. The first, which is the
creation of God, is purely good – in the creation of God
there is no evil; but the acquired capacity has become
the cause of the appearance of evil. For example, God
has created all men in such a manner and has given
them such a constitution and such capacities that they
are benefitted by sugar and honey and harmed and
destroyed by poison. This nature and constitution is
innate, and God has given it equally to all mankind.
But man begins little by little to accustom himself to

poison by taking a small quantity each day, and gradually increasing it, until he reaches such a point that he cannot live without a gram of opium every day. The natural capacities are thus completely perverted. Observe how much the natural capacity and constitution can be changed, until by different habits and training they become entirely perverted. One does not criticize vicious people because of their innate capacities and nature, but rather for their acquired capacities and nature.

In creation there is no evil; all is good. Certain qualities and natures innate in some men and apparently blameworthy are not so in reality. For example, from the beginning of his life you can see in a nursing child the signs of greed, of anger and of temper. Then, it may be said, good and evil are innate in the reality of man, and this is contrary to the pure goodness of nature and creation. The answer to this is that greed, which is to ask for something more, is a praiseworthy quality provided that it is used suitably. So if a man is greedy to acquire science and knowledge, or to become compassionate, generous and just, it is most praiseworthy. If he exercises his anger and wrath against the bloodthirsty tyrants who are like ferocious beasts, it is very praiseworthy; but if he does not use these qualities in a right way, they are blameworthy.[39]

'Abdu'l-Bahá

Although it is necessary for man to strive for material needs and comforts, his real need is the acquisition of the bounties of God. If he is bereft of divine bounties, spiritual susceptibilities and heavenly glad tidings, the life of man in this world has not yielded any worthy fruit. While possessing physical life, he should lay hold of the life spiritual, and together with bodily comforts and happiness, he should enjoy divine pleasures and content. Then is man worthy of the title man; then will he be after the image and likeness of God, for the image of the Merciful consists of the attributes of the heavenly Kingdom. If no fruits of the Kingdom appear in the garden of his soul, man is not in the image and likeness of God, but if those fruits are forthcoming, he becomes the recipient of ideal bestowals and is enkindled with the fire of the love of God.[40]

'Abdu'l-Bahá

Joy gives us wings! In times of joy our strength is more vital, our intellect keener . . .[41]

'Abdu'l-Bahá

. . . man should know his own self, and recognize that which leadeth unto loftiness or lowliness, glory or abasement, wealth or poverty.[42]

Bahá'u'lláh

Thankfulness is of various kinds. There is a verbal thanksgiving which is confined to a mere utterance of gratitude. This is of no importance because perchance the tongue may give thanks while the heart is unaware of it. Many who offer thanks to God are of this type, their spirits and hearts unconscious of thanksgiving. This is mere usage, just as when we meet, receive a gift and say thank you, speaking the words without significance. One may say thank you a thousand times while the heart remains thankless, ungrateful. Therefore, mere verbal thanksgiving is without effect. But real thankfulness is a cordial giving of thanks from the heart. When man in response to the favours of God manifests susceptibilities of conscience, the heart is happy, the spirit is exhilarated. These spiritual susceptibilities are ideal thanksgiving.

There is a cordial thanksgiving, too, which expresses itself in the deeds and actions of man when his heart is filled with gratitude. For example, God has conferred upon man the gift of guidance, and in thankfulness for this great gift certain deeds must emanate from him. To express his gratitude for the favours of God man must show forth praiseworthy actions. In response to these bestowals he must render good deeds, be self-sacrificing, loving the servants of God, forfeiting even life for them, showing kindness to all the creatures. He must be severed from the world, attracted to the Kingdom of Abhá, the face radiant, the tongue eloquent, the ear attentive, striving day and night to attain the good pleasure of God. Whatsoever he wishes to do must be in harmony with the good pleasure of God. He must observe and see what is the will of God and act accordingly. There can be no doubt that such commendable deeds are thankfulness for the favours of God.[43]

'Abdu'l-Bahá

Supreme happiness is man's, and he beholds the signs of God in the world and in the human soul, if he urges on the steed of high endeavour in the arena of civilization and justice.[44]

'Abdu'l-Bahá

References

The following translations have been used for references in this book. Old Testament, from *The Holy Scriptures*, According to the Masoretic Text (Philadelphia: The Jewish Publication Society of America, 1955). New Testament, from *The Holy Bible*, Authorized Version of 1611. Qur'án, from *The Koran*, translated by J.M. Rodwell (New York: Everyman's Library, 1909).

Creation

1. Bhagavad-Gita, *Hindu Scriptures*, edited and translated by R.C. Zaehner (New York: Everyman's Library, 1966), p. 286.
2. *The Dhammapada*, translated by P. Lal (New York: Farrar Straus and Giroux, 1967), v.
3. Digha-nikaya, I.235 (Tevijja Sutta), cited in Fozdar, Jamshed, *Buddha Maitrya-Amitabha Has Appeared* (New Delhi: Bahá'í Publishing Trust, 1976), p. 44.
4. Genesis 1:1.
5. Psalms 8:4–10.
6. Revelation 1:8.
7. John 1:1–4.
8. Surih 16:9–19.
9. Surih 78:1–16.
10. Surih 14:66–7.
11. Surih 67:3.

12. Bahá'u'lláh, *Gleanings from the Writings of Bahá'u'lláh* (Wilmette, Illinois: Bahá'í Publishing Trust, 1983), pp. 162–3.

13. ibid. pp. 64–5.

Prayer

1. Rig-Veda, *The Vedic Experience*, edited and translated by Raimundo Panikkar (Los Angeles: University of California Press, 1977), p. 72.

2. ibid. p. 857.

3. Atharva-Veda, in ibid., p. 299.

4. The Larger Sukhavati-Vyuha, 39, cited in Fozdar, *Buddha*, p. 463.

5. *Dhammapada* (Lal), vii, v. 96.

6. Psalms 105:1-4.

7. Psalms 67:2–8.

8. Psalms 51:12–14.

9. Numbers 6:24–6.

10. Psalms 25:1–6.

11. Luke 11:9–10.

12. Matthew 6:9–13.

13. Matthew 5:3–9, 16.

14. Surih 20:132.

15. Surih 2:147–8.

16. Surih 31:15–16.

17. Surih 1:1–6.

18. Surih 39:39.

19. Bahá'u'lláh, *Gleanings*, p. 295.

20. 'Abdu'l-Bahá, cited in *Bahá'í World Faith* (Wilmette, Illinois: Bahá'í Publishing Trust, 1971), p. 368.

21. Esslemont, J.E., *Bahá'u'lláh and the New Era* (Wil-

mette, Illinois: Bahá'í Publishing Trust, 5th rev. edn. 1980), pp. 85–6.
22. 'Abdu'l-Bahá in *Family Life*, compiled by the Research Department of the Universal House of Justice (Oakham: Bahá'í Publishing Trust, 1982), p. 8.
23. Bahá'u'lláh, *Kitáb-i-Íqán* (Wilmette, Illinois: Bahá'í Publishing Trust, rev. edn. 1974), p. 39.
24. Bahá'u'lláh in *Bahá'í Prayers* (Wilmette, Illinois: Bahá'í Publishing Trust, 1982), p. 204.
25. ibid. p. 141.
26. The Báb in ibid. p. 28.
27. Bahá'u'lláh in ibid. frontispiece.

Meditation

1. Chandogya Upanishad, *Hindu Scriptures*, p. 116.
2. Bhagavad-Gita, ibid. p. 283.
3. Kena Upanishad, *The Upanishads*, translated by Juan Mascaró (Harmondsworth, Middlesex: Penguin Books, 1965), p. 51.
4. *Dhammapada* (Lal), p. 134.
5. ibid. xiv, v. 188, p. 53.
6. ibid. viii, v. 111, p. 38.
7. ibid. p. 45.
8. ibid. p. 111.
9. *Sayings of Buddha*, translated by Justin Hartley Moore (New York: Columbia University Press, 1908), p. 36.
10. Joshua, 1:8–9.
11. Psalms 19:15.
12. Psalms 1:1–3.
13. Psalms 23:1–6.
14. Psalms 100:1–5.

15. Psalms 121:1–8.
16. Philippians 4:8.
17. James 1:5–8.
18. Luke 6:31.
19. Galatians 5:22–3.
20. Matthew 5:43–8.
21. Mark 4:30–2.
22. Surih 38:28.
23. Surih 13:12.
24. Surih 59:23–4.
25. Surih 4:151.
26. Surih 50:15–17.
27. Bahá'u'lláh, *Kitáb-i-Íqán*, p. 8.
28. 'Abdu'l-Bahá, *Paris Talks* (Wilmette, Illinois: Bahá'í Publishing Trust, rev. edn. 1989), pp. 160–2.
29. 'Abdu'l-Bahá, *The Promulgation of Universal Peace* (Wilmette, Illinois: Bahá'í Publishing Trust, rev. edn. 1982), p. 310.
30. Bahá'u'lláh, *Kitáb-i-Íqán*, p. 191.
31. Nabíl-i-A'zam, *The Dawn-Breakers* (Wilmette, Illinois: Bahá'í Publishing Trust, 1932), p. 94.

Faith

1. Bhagavad-Gita, *Hindu Scriptures*, p. 265.
2. Rig-Veda, *Vedic Experience*, p. 180.
3. Bhagavad-Gita, *Hindu Scriptures*, p. 270.
4. *Dhammapada* (Lal), p. 140.
5. ibid. p. 107.
6. Psalms 31:2–6.
7. Micah 4:2–5.
8. Matthew 17:20.
9. Luke 12:27–10.
10. Mark 9:23.

11. Romans 12:2–3.
12. Hebrews 11:1.
13. Surih 2:26–7.
14. Surih 13:2.
15. 'Abdu'l-Bahá, *Paris Talks*, p. 94.
16. 'Abdu'l-Bahá in *The Divine Art of Living* (Wilmette, Illinois: Bahá'í Publishing Trust, rev. edn. 1960), p. 48.

Unity

1. Bhagavad-Gita, *Hindu Scriptures*, p. 306.
2. ibid. p. 272.
3. Atharva-Veda, *Vedic Experience*, p. 857.
4. *The Dhammapada, The Path of Perfection*, translated by Juan Mascaró (Harmondsworth, Middlesex: Penguin Books, 1973), p. 54.
5. Buddhacarita, vv. 1522–30, cited in Fozdar, *Buddha*.
6. Vinaya-pitaka, I.20, ibid.
7. Sutta-nipata, vv. 149–50, ibid.
8. Psalms 133:1.
9. Isaiah 32:15–17.
10. Matthew 12:25.
11. Romans 12:9–18.
12. Surih 2:81.
13. Surih 5:120.
14. Bahá'u'lláh, *Gleanings*, p. 95.
15. 'Abdu'l-Bahá, *Promulgation*, p. 24.
16. ibid. p. 32.

Love

1. Bhagavad-Gita, *Hindu Scriptures*, p. 302.
2. *Dhammapada* (Lal), p. 39.
3. *Sayings of Buddha*, p. 39.

4. *Dhammapada* (Lal), xvii, v. 223.
5. ibid. xv. c. 197.
6. Deuteronomy 30:16.
7. Deuteronomy 6:4–7.
8. Proverbs 8:17–21.
9. Matthew 22:37–40.
10. John 3:16.
11. I Corinthians 13:1–13.
12. I John 4:7–8.
13. I John 4:12.
14. John 15:9–13.
15. I John 4:16.
16. I Corinthians 2:9–12.
17. Surih 19:96.
18. Surih 17:24–6.
19. Surih 42:22.
20. 'Abdu'l-Bahá, *Paris Talks*, pp. 165–7.
21. 'Abdu'l-Bahá, *Selections from the Writings of 'Abdu'l-Bahá* (Haifa: Bahá'í World Centre, 1978), p. 27.
22. 'Abdu'l-Bahá, *Promulgation*, p. 15.
23. ibid. p. 348.
24. ibid. p. 8.
25. 'Abdu'l-Bahá in *Bahá'í World Faith*, p. 364.

Guidance

1. Bhagavad-Gita, *Hindu Scriptures*, p. 279.
2. ibid. p. 263.
3. ibid. p. 273.
4. Katha Upanishad, *Hindu Scriptures*, p. 176.
5. *Dhammapada* (Lal), p. 65.
6. *Sayings of Buddha*, p. 102.
7. *Dhammapada* (Lal), p. 93.
8. Psalms 73:24–6.

9. Isaiah 40:28–31.
10. Proverbs 3:13–24.
11. Matthew 4:4.
12. Matthew 19:19.
13. Matthew 24:35.
14. Galatians 6:3–7.
15. Matthew 13:1–9.
16. Luke 15:11–32.
17. Ephesians 6:14–17.
18. Luke 6:35–8.
19. Ephesians 6:1–4.
20. Acts 20:35.
21. I John 4:18–21.
22. Ephesians 5:25–33.
23. Surih 39:7–10.
24. Surih 31:30–34
25. Surih 46:12–18.
26. Surih 28:56.
27. Surih 24:35.
28. Surih 2:1–4.
29. Surih 29:68.
30. Surih 11:113.
31. Bahá'u'lláh, *Kitáb-i-Íqán*, pp. 240–1.
32. Bahá'u'lláh, *Tablets of Bahá'u'lláh* (Haifa: Bahá'í World Centre, 1978), p. 156.
33. ibid. p. 36.
34. Bahá'u'lláh, *Gleanings*, p. 260.
35. ibid. p. 250.
36. The Báb, *Selections from the Writings of the Báb* (Haifa: Bahá'í World Centre, 1976), p. 80.
37. 'Abdu'l-Bahá, *Promulgation*, pp. 144–5.
38. 'Abdu'l-Bahá, *Selections*, p. 299.
39. 'Abdu'l-Bahá, *Some Answered Questions* (Wilmette, Illinois: Bahá'í Publishing Trust, 1981), p. 214.

40. 'Abdu'l-Bahá, *Promulgation*, p. 335.
41. 'Abdu'l-Bahá, *Paris Talks*, p. 95.
42. Bahá'u'lláh, *Tablets*, p. 35.
43. 'Abdu'l-Bahá, *Promulgation*, p. 236.
44. 'Abdu'l-Bahá, *The Secret of Divine Civilization* (Wilmette, Illinois: Bahá'í Publishing Trust, 1957), p. 4.